BECOMING THE BELOVED

The End-Time Bride of Christ

To Vince
Live Life Loved!

MARK DAVIDSON

Shulamite Ministries Publishing

Proofread by: Betty Vander Linden
Edited by: Querida Duncalfe

Printed in the United States of America 2010
Second Printing in the United States of America 2013

ISBN: 978-0-578-04812-3

CONTENTS

For Rebecca, my own "Beloved"

PREFACE

It helps in a pinch to be able to remind your bride
that you gave up a throne for her.
Edward, Duke of Windsor

A King's Ransom

One of the most remarkable love stories of all time involved the abdication of a throne. In 1936, King Edward VIII gave up his right of ascension to marry a divorced American named Wallis Simpson. He did so over the stern objections of the British government, the Royal Family and the Church of England. As the romance between Edward and his lover burgeoned, Wallis' sullied reputation became fodder for scandal. The controversy grew until it became clear to Edward that to have the woman he loved he would have to leave his throne. On December 11, 1936, he did just that when he submitted his formal abdication in writing after occupying the throne for only eleven months. In doing so, he renounced forever the unique privilege, power and birthright afforded by the throne. At that moment his brother became England's king and the lesser title of Duke of Windsor was bestowed upon Edward. The news rocked the world and has since become an enduring testimony to the compelling power of passionate desire.

A Lovesick King

In some ways, this love story is very much like the eternal love story of Jesus and His own Bride. To have the one *He* loved, He also had to abdicate His throne. The Bible says,

> *[He] made Himself of no reputation, taking the form of a bondservant, and coming in the likeness of men.*[1]

Theologians call this act of abdication the "kenosis,"[2] which means "to empty oneself of position and authority". Like Edward, Jesus also chose to relinquish the heavenly throne in order to have His own "scandalous" Bride. The dark blemish of our sinful nature did not dissuade our lovesick King in His passionate pursuit of us. Many have been taught that salvation is a demonstration of God's pity. *There is no love story in that!* He did not save us because He pitied us. He saved us because He *desired us!*

The Most Excellent Love Song

About one thousand years before the birth of Christ, yet another love story blossomed in Israel. The romance of Solomon and his bride, called the Shulamite, is described in breathtaking detail in the book of the Bible called the *Song of Songs*. In Hebrew, Solomon's beautiful masterpiece is called the "Shir ha'Shirim," which means *"The Most Excellent Song."* There are ten notable songs in the Bible which were revered by the ancient Jews.[3] They include such anthems as the victory song of Moses[4] as well as the song of Deborah and Barak.[5] Compared with these, the *Song of Songs* was deemed superlative to them all, because it was viewed as the most profound revelation of God's love for His people.

---

[1] Philippians 2:7 RSV

[2] Greek

[3] These ten songs are called "Israel's Songs of Renown"

[4] Exodus 15:1

[5] Judges 5:1

A Holy Enigma

Today, the *Song of Songs* remains one of the least studied and least understood books in the Bible. It is an ancient enigma which has baffled and intrigued believers down through the ages. On the surface it appears to be little more than a love poem consisting mainly of a dialogue between Solomon and the Shulamite. Below the water-mark, however, lie hidden treasures of amazing revelation! In the little book of only 8 chapters and 117 verses, Solomon ensconces the deeper truths of the book in clever symbols, archetypes and allegory. He does so as a means of concealing the true riches of the book. Like all hidden treasures, only those who diligently seek them will find them.

Why This Book?

Part One of this book is a call to believers everywhere to begin to experience a deeper, more intimate relationship with Christ. In an effort to unlock the secrets of this romantic tale, I share things I have learned from my own study of the *Song* as well as insights gleaned from hours of contemplative prayer. In *Part Two*, I address the events of the Last Days. I do so because the emergence of the Bride is an event clearly reserved for the days preceding the return of Christ. With prophetic portents of current world events pointing to the imminent return of the Bridegroom, many are now beginning to contemplate their identity and destiny as the Bride of Christ. To this I can only say:

"Even so, Come, Lord Jesus!"

PART ONE

1

THE MYSTERY

We speak of God's secret wisdom, a wisdom that has been hidden and that God destined for our glory before time began.
1 Corinthians 2:7

A Good Mystery

Like most people, I love a good mystery, and the Bible offers up one particular mystery that is both profoundly beautiful and beautifully profound. It is called the *Mystery of the Bride.*[6] By definition, a spiritual mystery is certain knowledge that is concealed by God until the appropriate time. Daniel, for example, was told to "shut up" the words of his vision and to "seal the book" of his prophecy *until* the end of time.[7] As a result, an unseen veil has covered his words until now. In the same way, the *Mystery of the Bride,* although a significant theme of the Bible, has largely been misunderstood, marginalized and sometimes even maligned down through the centuries because it too is a revelation that cannot be fully fathomed until the right time.

A Mega Mystery

In Ephesians 5, the Apostle Paul draws special attention to the *Mystery of the Bride* by calling it a "great" mystery. The word "great" in the Greek language is the word "mega" and it refers to

---

[6] See Eph. 5:32
[7] See Daniel 12:4

something that is "superior in dimension, grandeur or rank." In the same way King Solomon's ode to his bride is considered superlative to all other songs, the *Mystery of the Bride* is held forth as the most significant mystery of all spiritual mysteries. While a total of at least twelve such mysteries are revealed in the New Testament, the *Mystery of the Bride* is right at the top of the list. Indeed, it is God's mega-mystery!

A Woman of Mystery

The supreme climactic moment of human history will occur when the Bride of Christ debuts upon the world stage. The apocalyptic events of the book of Revelation all culminate in a singular event called the "Marriage of the Lamb." This future celestial ceremony will be the crowning conclusion and the zenith of God's redemptive plan for mankind. In the days just preceding the return of Jesus to judge the world, this *woman of mystery* called the "Lamb's wife,"[8] will emerge from obscurity to take her appointed place in the unfolding drama of the Last Days. Then, the mystery that has been hidden from the beginning of Creation will be seen and understood at last. Who is this "mystery woman?" Who is this whose simple gaze can conquer the Conqueror and "ravish the heart of God?"[9] Who is this of who it is said "the King is enthralled by your beauty?"[10] *Answering these questions forms the very basis of this book.*

The Seal of Solomon

No other book of the Bible reveals more about the *Mystery of the Bride* than does the *Song of Songs*. Like the book of Daniel, the full depth of the meaning of the *Song* has long been "shut up

---

[8] Revelation 21:9
[9] Song of Songs 4:9
[10] Psalm 45:11

and sealed" until the appropriate time. The following declaration appears three times in the *Song:*

> "I adjure you, O daughters of Jerusalem, by the gazelles or by the hinds of the field, that you do not arouse or awaken my love until she pleases."[11]

I believe these words, spoken by Solomon some three thousand years ago, placed a "divine seal" upon the deeper meaning of the *Song*. Interestingly, the seal was not placed directly upon the *words* of the *Song* itself. Rather, it was placed upon the *heart and mind* of the Bride! She has been kept from experiencing the deep, intimate love of God until she is ready. By nature, gazelles and deer (hinds) are delicate, sensitive creatures easily roused and startled. The fact that they are invoked in this thrice-spoken declaration refers to the delicate nature of the Bridal revelation. While the *compassionate* nature of the love of Father God is something easily entreated by most people, the *passionate* nature of the love of Jesus for His Bride is not. Thinking of God as a romantic lover is not an easy concept for most people to grasp, yet this is exactly how the Bible presents Him.

Ready for Love and a Lover

In the 16th chapter of Ezekiel, a beautiful picture of God choosing Israel as His Bride is found. In the parable set forth by the prophet, God first came to Israel when she was just a baby. Cast out and rejected by everyone, God found her and saved her from certain death:

> On the day you were born your umbilical cord was not cut, you weren't bathed and cleaned up, you weren't

[11] Song of Songs 2:7 NASB

> rubbed with salt, you weren't wrapped in a baby blanket. No one cared a fig for you. No one did one thing to care for you tenderly in these ways. You were thrown out into a vacant lot and left there, dirty and unwashed—a newborn nobody wanted. And then I came by. I saw you all miserable and bloody. Yes, I said to you, lying there helpless and filthy, "Live!"[12]

Time passed and the baby grew into a beautiful young woman. She became tall and her breasts were formed. When God passed by her the *second time* he exclaimed:

> I came by again and saw you, saw that you were ready for love and a lover. I took care of you, dressed you and protected you. I promised you my love and entered the covenant of marriage with you.[13] [emphasis added]

Beloved, two thousand years ago Jesus passed by the field of the world and found us lost and dying. Through His sacrificial death he proclaimed to all mankind, "Live!" Now, as the end of the age fast approaches, Jesus is passing by His people yet again. This time He comes to see if we have matured and reached the time when we are "ready for love and a lover." This secondary encounter with Christ is depicted beautifully in the *Song of Songs* where the king "goes down" to His garden to see if the fruit has reached the stage of maturity. The imagery of the king going "down" into the garden is an allusion to Christ coming down from heaven to earth at the end of the age.

---

[12] Ezekiel 16:4-7 The Message

[13] Ezekiel 16:8-14 The Message

> I went down into the garden of nuts to see the fruits of the valley, and to see whether the vine flourished and the pomegranates budded[14]

Christ is not returning for a Church that resembles an immature girl. He is returning for a womanly Bride. Romantic love is not meant for children. For a girl to be ready for intimacy, her body must change. Her hips must widen, and her breasts must form. So it is with the "Body" of Christ. Until we are willing to put away our perpetual pubescence, we will never awaken to the high calling of becoming God's Bride.

Sleeping Beauty

For many today, the seal that has restrained our hearts from fully comprehending our destiny to *Become the Beloved* is finally breaking away. We are awakening to the call to rise above the status quo malaise of modern Christianity. We feel the restless need to experience an emotional connection to the beating heart of Christ. It is not another sermon *about* the love of God that we need or want; it is an actual experience *with* the love of God that we seek. The Church is much like a "sleeping beauty." Our hearts are asleep in the contentment of our salvation. Multitudes of believers have no desire whatsoever to know God in ways that are deeply intimate. For them, being saved is reward enough. Others, however, who comprise a growing remnant, have glimpsed a greater reward. Their hearts have awakened to the possibility of an experience of love so intimate and infused with God's affection that it requires a bridal covenant to indulge!

---

[14] Song of Songs 6:11

Leaving Our Comfort Zone

In the love story of the *Song of Songs,* the emerging Bride of Christ is pre-figured in the person of Solomon's bride. In chapter 3, we read where she must leave the comfort of her bed and the contentment of sleep to pursue her lover:

> Restless in bed and sleepless through the night, I longed for my lover. I wanted him desperately. His absence was painful. So, I got up, went out and roved the city, hunting through streets and down alleys. I wanted my lover in the worst way![15]

Have you felt yourself drawn away from the contentment of things familiar? Do Christian "concerts and conferences" no longer sate the deeper need of your soul? Has His absence in your life become painful? Is your "comfort zone" no longer all that comfortable? Rest assured it is the Spirit of God that works in you to make you restless until you are "ready for love and your lover!"[16]

---

[15] Song of Songs 3:1-3 The Message

[16] Ezekiel 16:8 The Message

2
THE END TIME BRIDE

For everything there is a season and a time
for every purpose under heaven.
The Book of Ecclesiastes

The Remnant Bride

While the concept of being the Bride of God is deeply rooted in the theology of both the Old and New Testaments, it remains undiscovered by much of the Church today. The popular belief is that the Church and the Bride is the same thing. Near the end of time, however, a clear distinction between the two will be seen. This dissimilarity of the two is evidenced by the fact that the word "church" is not even found beyond the 3rd chapter of the book of Revelation! Instead, the people of God are called the "Lamb's wife"[17] or the "Bride."[18] Problematic eschatological[19] paradigms with their confusing charts and timelines become more easily understood once the Bride is viewed as something separate from the Church.

The Bride is called a "mystery" because she has existed as a hidden remnant of people within the greater Body of Christ since the Day of Pentecost two thousand years ago. The mystery of her existence will be understood only when she becomes discernibly distinct from the Church during the Last Days. It is safe to say that the Bride of Christ is an end-time phenomenon.

---

[17] Revelation 21:9
[18] Revelation 22:10
[19] Eschatology is the study of the events of the End of Days.

Her hidden nature becomes manifest only briefly right before Jesus returns to take her out of the world and to her wedding.

The Sixth Day

To understand the prophetic timing of the Bride's appearance just before the return of Christ, it helps to look at the way this mystery has been foretold in Scripture.

Numbers play an important part in Biblical interpretation and the number *six* represents the history of mankind from beginning to end. Think of the seven days of the week as a microcosm of all of world history. According to the Jewish Talmud,[20] the literal days of the week represent 1,000 year periods of time.[21] Although science speculates that the earth is billions of years old, there is a growing body of solid scientific evidence to the contrary.[22] Jewish theology clearly teaches that God has allotted a fixed period of 6,000 years to mankind. Once that time has elapsed, the world will end. Then, Messiah will appear on the "seventh day" (the Great Sabbath) to set up His literal kingdom on earth. His earthly reign will last another thousand years. Christian theology agrees with this view and calls this 1,000 year epoch of time the "millennial reign of Christ."

The Law Concerning Slaves

The significance of the number six can be found throughout the Bible. According to Jewish law, for example, slaves were to be given their freedom after serving a total of *six* years.[23] In a larger sense, this speaks of all mankind which has been held

---

[20] The Talmud is a record of rabbinic discussions pertaining to Jewish law and ethics.
[21] SANHEDRIN 97A4 52
[22] See Young Earth Creationism (YEC)
[23] Exodus 21:2

in bondage to sin and death for *6,000* years. Mankind's spiritual slavery will be abolished in totality at the end of the sixth day!

Six Measures of Barley

In the allegorical book of Ruth, we find another interesting occurrence of the number six as a representation of time. Ruth, who is a Gentile, gleans in the harvest field of a benevolent land owner named Boaz. She represents the complete human race from the beginning of time. This is symbolized when she brings a gift of *six* measures of barley which she gives to Naomi, her *Jewish* mother-in-law.[24] Here is the meaning: When the spiritual harvest of the earth is complete (6 full measures), then the "times of the Gentiles" will end. Then, the Gentiles will hand the harvest over to the Jews once more! Naomi represents the Jewish people who become the recipients of the final spiritual harvest at the end of time.[25]

In The New Testament

The idea of days representing millennia is supported in the New Testament as well. The Apostle Peter, for example, wrote,

> "With God, a single day is as a thousand years."[26]

Also, in the account of the transfiguration of Jesus, we read:

> Now after six days, Jesus took Peter, James, and John his brother, led them up on a high mountain by themselves; and He was transfigured before them. His face shone like

---

[24] Ruth 3:11-15

[25] See the chapter titled "The Last Harvest" to learn more.

[26] 2 Peter 3:8

the sun, and His clothes became as white as the light.[27] [emphasis added]

Almost all scholars agree that this event was a pre-figuring of the *future glorification* of Christ in the age to come.[28] By using the phrase "after six days," the Spirit pinpointed the future historical timing of the physical return of Jesus in His future glory! Christ will be seen in His ascended glory *after the sixth day* (6,000 years) of human history.

Six Water Pots

Consider as well the first miracle that Jesus performed. It was at a wedding. He arrived in the midst of the celebration and was told they were out of wine. When His mother asked Him to do something, He told her "My hour has not yet come."[29] The "hour" He was referring to was the hour of His *own* wedding.

According to Jewish custom, the bridegroom was responsible for providing all the wine for the wedding party, and this was *not* Jesus' wedding! However, Jesus used the occasion as a "teaching moment" by asking that *six* water pots be filled to the brim. Not five. Not seven. Six! After this was done, He turned the water into wine. The meaning is clear. When 6,000 years have elapsed (represented by the six jars filled to the brim) the hour of Jesus' own wedding *will* come, and then He *will* provide the wine!

The Bride is Formed on the Sixth Day

In the account of Creation, we find our final example of the prophetic use of the number six when we read that Adam's bride

---

[27] Matthew 17:1-2
[28] See 2 Peter 1:16
[29] John 2:4 RSV

was formed at the end of the *sixth* day or *at the end of the week!* Likewise, the Bride of the "last Adam"[30] (Christ) will also come forth on the "sixth day" of human history – or at the end of time! How exciting that the Bride is indeed emerging in our generation!

What Time Is It?

Despite what we might believe concerning the actual age of the earth, we might be wise to consider the prophetic significance of the Jewish calendar as it relates to the dispensation of God's plan for mankind.[31] A famous 4th century rabbi, named Hillel II, created a fixed calendar which he based on the cycles of the moon. His calendar ends at the year 6,000! He did not calculate beyond that point because he believed that after the year 6,000 a new era of time would begin which is called the Shabbat HaGadol (the Great Sabbath.) According to Hillel's calendar, the current year at the writing of this book is 5,770.[32] As you can see, only 230 years remain in this final millennium. However, it should be noted that some Jewish scholars contend that Hillel's calendar is under-calculated by 165 years. *If this is true, then Jesus is literally at the door!*

The Messiah Movement in Israel

While this knowledge remains hidden from most of the world, many Jews in Israel today are feverishly preparing for the appearance of their Messiah and the end of the world. While the

---

[30] 1 Corinthians 15:45 Here Jesus is called "the last Adam".

[31] The reader might wish to read the book *Thousands Not Millions: Challenging the Icon of Evolution, Questioning the Age of the Earth* by Donald DeYoung. Masters Books.

[32] There is some debate over the accuracy of the Jewish calendar, however, the number of months in question are inconsequential to the fact that we are now living in the final allotted days of human history if this viewpoint is correct.

world measures time by the sun calendar,[33] they watch the *moon* and are well aware that the 6,000 years promised to them by God is fast coming to an end! Jewish religious organizations such as the Temple Mount Faithful[34] and the Temple Institute[35] are actively preparing for the end of the world and the coming of the Messiah. And indeed, the "messiah" they look for *will* appear and right on time! He will not be the deliverer they yearn for, however. He will be the Anti-Christ masquerading as their deliverer. Despite the treaty he makes with them, ultimately he will seek to destroy them.

---

[33] Gregorian calendar
[34] See www.templemountfaithful.org
[35] See www.templeinstitute.org

3

OF SERVANTS AND BRIDES

If I must die, I will encounter darkness as a bride,
and hug it in mine arms.
William Shakespeare

Two Answers to One Question

One of the most intriguing parables told by Jesus is that of the wise and foolish virgins.[36] It is told in response to a question asked by the disciples concerning what signs would signal His return and the end of the world.[37] He answered their question by telling them two stories in which he described two very different types of people who will be waiting for His return. In the first parable, Jesus spoke of brides waiting for their bridegroom. In the second story, He described servants waiting for their master to return from a long journey to give them their pay. Jesus chose to answer the question by giving two examples and not just one because there will indeed be two distinct kinds of people awaiting His return – *servants and brides!*

---

[36] Matthew 25
[37] The question posed by the disciples is found in Matthew 24:3

The Superior Reward

In both parables, each type of believer receives a reward. The servants receive the right to reign in God's coming kingdom. Their reward is, in essence, a continuation of the same kind of master/servant relationship they had with God on earth. They ruled over a little and now they will rule over much. The Bride's reward, however, is the *Bridegroom Himself!*

God recognizes and honors both His servants and His Bride. Both will receive their expected rewards. The far superior reward, however, is reserved for those who possess a Bridal heart. As the end of the age draws near, we must choose which kind of people we will be. *Will we be servants or will we be brides?*

Here Comes the Bride

Presently a small but significant "bridal" company of men and women are beginning to arise all over the world. They are distinguished by their passionate and devoted pursuit of knowing God intimately. They feel not only called to salvation but *chosen* to participate in the unfolding events of the Last Days as well. They gaze longingly for the imminent return of Jesus and hasten His coming with their longing prayer. To this holy company, the Marriage of the Lamb is something that is becoming more than a vague theological concept. To them it is becoming their future reality. This alone is a clear fulfillment of what Jesus foretold in the parable of the wise and foolish maidens!

> Then [at the end of the age] the kingdom of heaven shall be likened to ten virgins who took their lamps and went out to meet the bridegroom.[38] [emphasis added]

---

[38] Matthew 25:1 RSV

When asked what would portend the end of the world, Jesus said that one sign to look for was the emergence of the Bride herself! This means that Jesus will *not* return *until* His Bride comes forth as a definable company of people who await His return. Nor will He return *until* His Bride has been given a season in which to make herself ready to meet Him. In the book of Revelation, we read:

> Let us be glad and rejoice and exult and give Him glory, for the marriage of the Lamb has come, and His wife ***has made herself ready.*** (Revelation 19:7) [emphasis added]

No one can say how long this season of preparation will be, but there is little doubt that it has already begun. When we consider how world events are fulfilling biblical prophecy almost on a daily basis, it certainly signals an acceleration toward the End of Days. While much of the Church remains blasé concerning the coming of the Lord, the Bride is distinguished by the fact that she grows more joyfully expectant of her Bridegroom's return with each passing day.

Faithful Servant or Cherished Bride?

Often, when I am sharing this message with an audience, I make the statement that I personally have no desire to hear Jesus say to me, "Well done, good and faithful servant."[39] As you might imagine, this sparks instant controversy. We have been taught that these very words are the crowning epitaph of a life well lived for God. That is certainly true - *if one is a servant!* Brides, on the other hand, do not live for the approval of a master. *They live for the affections of their husband!*

In the *Song of Songs,* the first words uttered by the Bride

[39] Matthew 25:21

are, *"Let him kiss me with the kisses of his mouth!"*[40] She does not seek the lesser rewards of power, position or promotion. She seeks, instead, the *greater* reward of relationship, intimacy and affection.

What is Wrong with Being a Servant?

Some might argue, "What is wrong with being a servant? Didn't Jesus possess a servant's heart?" *Yes, He did.* Without argument, Jesus said of Himself, "the Son of man did not come to be served, but to serve."[41] He said that, however, as a way of exhorting His disciples to serve *one another.* Jesus was indeed a servant *to men.* But He was *never* a servant to His Father! To His Father, He was always a *Son!* In that sense, we too should seek to serve one another with a servant's heart. But in our relationship with Jesus, He is never our Master! *He is our Husband.*

Master or Bridegroom?

Because the "master/servant" model of Christianity is so widely taught and accepted today, the presentation of the Bridal paradigm often sparks controversy and resistance. The real question, however, is not, "How do we view God?" but rather, "How does God *wish* to be viewed?" With this in mind, consider the words of the prophet Hosea:

> And it shall be in that day, says the LORD, That you will call me, 'My husband,' [Ishi] and no longer call me, 'My Master' [Ba'al][42]

---

[40] Song of Songs 1:2
[41] Matthew 20:28
[42] Hosea 2:16

God did not deliver the children of Israel from 400 years of slavery to Pharaoh only to treat them the same way! *No!* He brought them out of bondage to bring them into a *love relationship*. God's greatest desire was that they know Him as intimately as a wife knows her husband! I believe many Christians today also see God as a master to be doggedly served rather than the loving Husband He really is.

When Hosea said "in that day" he made reference to a *future* time when the very thought of God, as a master, would be taken from the hearts and minds of His people. That future day finally arrived when Jesus offered Israel a New Covenant which reads:

> Behold, *the days are coming*, says the LORD, when I will make a new covenant with the house of Israel and the house of Judah, not according to the covenant that I made with their fathers in the day when I took them by the hand to lead them out of the land of Egypt, My covenant which they broke, *though I was a husband to them* says the LORD.[43] [emphasis added]

The words "though I was a husband to them" shows that God was Israel's husband all along! But they could not accept Him in that role. It was their *choice* to make Him into the likeness of the kind of master they had served in Egypt.

At the end of time, there will be those who sought a servant's reward and they will receive it. But I no longer live my life with the goal of hearing the words, "Well done good and faithful servant."[44] Ever since I began to comprehend my true identity as the Bride of Christ, He has ceased to be my "Ba'al." He

---

[43] Jeremiah 31:31
[44] Matthew 25:21

is now my "Ishi"- *my Husband!* And I have ceased to think of myself as His servant. Instead, I am His Bride - *His Beloved!*

Mary, Martha, and Performance Orientation

How do you perceive God? It is an important question since your future and destiny depends on how you answer! This is because our concept of God gives us our own self-concept as well. The image of God you carry in your mind ultimately shapes your very life and personality.

The story of Martha and Mary[45] illustrates and contrasts the difference between those who have a master/servant relationship with God and those who possess a Bridal heart. Martha clearly sought to please the Lord with her service, while Mary chose to sit at the feet of *Jesus* and receive *Him* as her reward. Mary is a figure of the Bride of Christ who views *relationship* as being the superior reward. A similar scene of simply resting at the feet of God is found in the *Song* when Solomon's bride says:

> Like an apple tree among the trees of the woods, So is my beloved among the sons. With great delight ***I sat in his shade, and his fruit was sweet to my taste.***[46] [emphasis added]

A Purpose Driven Life?

Certainly our lives should have purpose. But are we to be people who are *driven?* The very word "driven" connotes the life of a servant.

---

[45] Luke 10:38-42
[46] Song of Songs 2:3

While servants feel compelled to put their shoulder to the wheel and push their way dutifully through life, those who have been captured by the love of their Bridegroom feel no guilt whatsoever in "wasting" their time, attention and resources doing nothing more than basking in His presence.

Once we have discovered and experienced the superior reward of the pleasures of loving and being loved by our Bridegroom, lesser rewards will diminish in their appeal. Many believers, like Martha, are chained to a performance-oriented type of Christian living that drives them to seek approval from God. Those who are being apprehended as the Bride are not so. They are too love-struck to care about anything other than *being* with the One they love. This sacred kind of lovesickness threatens the very underpinnings of works-based religion and creates an uncomfortable tension between workers *for* God and lovers *of* God. I have discovered that there are two things in life that can take our breath away. One is by running as hard and as fast as we can. The other is being kissed with passion. *I choose the kiss!*

Wasting Time

At our church in Texas, there is a large prayer room we call "The King's Chamber." Lights are kept low and worship music plays continuously. Large comfortable pillows are scattered around the room, where people can come if they desire and "waste" their time in contemplative prayer and worship. But is it truly wasted time? Is it wasted time when lovers spend countless hours just *being* together? *Of course not!* The Christian life is not just about working *for* God; it is also about building an intimate love relationship *with* Him. Time spent with God is *never* wasted time. In fact, it seems to me that with all of our *doing,* we are not really comfortable with just *being.*

My Personal Story

I first came to Jesus when I was a teenager. From that time forward, I cannot recall ever hearing any teaching that presented Jesus in the role of my Bridegroom. He was presented as my Savior, Lord, King and Master; but *never once* as my Husband. Even after being involved in full-time Christian ministry as a pastor and teacher for nearly twenty years, I still had no concept of Christ in that important role. That would all change when, in 2002, my wife and I took some time away from ministry to devote ourselves to a season of seeking the Lord for personal renewal. We met with our church's leadership team to discuss the possibility of taking a sabbatical. When we left that meeting, I think we all thought our time away would last only a couple of weeks or perhaps a month at most.

On the first day of my sabbatical, I entered the prayer room at our church with an honest desire to seek the Lord for a fresh revelation of who He is. I had no real plan or agenda beyond that. I recall walking to the center of the room, sitting on the floor and then simply asking God to lead and help me. After waiting quietly for awhile, I opened my Bible and it fell open to the *Song of Songs*. In a short space of time, I had read the entire book and, like the words of John Wesley, "I felt my heart was strangely warmed."[47] From that moment, I was drawn into a revelation of the *Song* which would ultimately change my life and ministry. The short sabbatical period I had planned ended up lasting *almost a year!* During that time I did not teach or speak publically. Instead I devoted myself to prayer and a study of the *Song of Songs*.

---

[47] From John Wesley's Journal in which he described his experience of being filled with the assurance of his salvation.

In the course of that "wasted" year, God poured more into me than the twenty years that preceded it!

A Revelation that Caused a Revolution

I must admit that I had always found the *Song of Songs* a difficult book to understand. Like many people, I had neglected it. But on *that* particular day and at *that* precise moment, God met me in a way that was so powerfully intimate it became one of the few authentic life-changing experiences of my life. The words of the *Song* suddenly seemed as if they had been written just for me. For the first time in my life I began to understand more fully *why* God had saved me, and it was not just to give me a home in heaven. It was so He might draw me into a fiery, holy experience of love so powerful as to cause the two of us to become inseparably one. It was a *revelation* that would lead to nothing short of a total *revolution* of my Christian life. As I began my own journey toward understanding God's affection for me as His Bride, it replaced the unworthiness I felt with a secure sense of total acceptance.

Our Image of God

Some of what I have written within these pages is understandably subjective because it is born out of my personal encounters with God. On the other hand, we should remember that the Bible is not merely a rule-book comprised of principles and precepts; rather, it is an enthralling *storybook* about how real flesh-and-blood men and women literally encountered the God of the Word *subjectively.*

We form our image of God based on what we have been taught about Him as well as how He has been interpreted to us by our particular religious culture and tradition. To that we add our own ideas, which have been shaped by our life experiences. My own experiences over the last few years have led to a major restructuring of my concept of God as well as my understanding of the Scriptures. The revelation of Jesus as my Bridegroom has taken me far beyond my foundational understanding of Him as my Savior. For some people, imagining Jesus in the role of a passionate Bridegroom proves *too* intimate for their sensibilities. While it may indeed be more comfortable to cling to a *platonic* version of Jesus, we should never fear having our concepts of God challenged and refined as we grow in faith. If we are led by the Holy Spirit, He will ultimately lead us into all that is true about God.

Personal Theology

When we attempt to define God solely by what we have learned about Him from the Bible, we limit our comprehension of God to doctrinal truth. While essential to our faith, doctrinal truth *cannot* define what God is to each of us *personally*. Indeed, it was precisely the most astute scholars of the day who could not see Jesus in His true reality when He was standing right before them in the flesh! Paradoxically, they were blinded by their inflexible allegiance to doctrinal truth! This is a danger we still face today. Religion which denies having personal encounters with God leads to a rigid kind of fossilized spirituality. For our theology to be true it must first be *personal*. Unless we have first had an *encounter* with God, everything the Bible says about Him - while true - is no more than untested academic *theory*. As a Jew, Peter studied the Torah from a young age. His concept of God was based upon the perfection of the Law. But his knowledge of the Scriptures was not sufficient to reveal who Jesus was to him *personally*. Otherwise, Jesus would not have asked him the question: *"Who do you say that I am?"*[48]

---

[48] Matthew 16:15

Who God Is

Despite the biblically correct beliefs we dearly hold of God, our *true* God is simply, yet profoundly, defined by Jesus as that which we choose to *"love with all of our heart, soul, and might."*[49] A more literal translation of the word "might" is the word "abundance" (i.e. money.)

While it is vital that our understanding of God be undergirded by the truth of what the Bible says about Him, we should never lose sight of the fact that our real "God" is always that to which we direct our passions, pursuits and even something as mundane as our money. Ultimately, it is not what we *believe* that provides us a clear revelation of the living God; rather, it is to Whom we *cleave.*

---

[49] Deuteronomy 6:5

4

THE THEOLOGY OF ROMANCE

A romantic theologian does not mean one who is romantic about theology but one who is theological about romance.
C.S. Lewis

Love Stories

Many people are surprised to discover that the whole of the Word of God is wrapped around a romantic bridal theme. Once you discover just *how central* this theme really is, it might possibly change the way you read and understand the Bible forever.

We tend to think of the Old Testament in terms of the meticulous nature of the Mosaic Law, yet it is also replete with thrilling love stories! The timeless story of man's longing for a bride is told and re-told through the lives of biblical characters such as Adam and Eve, Isaac and Rebecca, Boaz and Ruth, Esther and the King, Hosea and Gomer, and Solomon and the Shulamite. Each of these tales lends a unique perspective to the larger story of God's love for His own Bride.

What is Bridal Theology?

"Bridal Theology" is a term used to describe a certain way of understanding the Scriptures in light of its dominant romantic theme. It is a perspective deeply rooted in the Old Testament, where the prophets often described Israel as God's Bride.[50] In the New Testament, this idea is amplified even more when Christ is presented as the literal embodiment of the long-awaited Bridegroom. While many theologians teach that the Bride of Christ is merely a metaphor, others feel it describes a spiritual reality which defines our covenant relationship with God.

The History of Bridal Theology

Bridal Theology did not *develop* as much as it was *discovered*. Solomon wrote 3,000 proverbs and 1,005 songs.[51] When he penned the *Song of Songs* 3,000 years ago, perhaps he meant it only as a love poem to his bride. Its mystique began to grow, however, when the ancient Jews added it to the liturgy of their Passover celebration. Over time, a special veneration of the *Song* evolved among Jews and Christians alike. Down through time, certain people discovered the real meaning of the book and were given glimpses of the truth contained in the mysterious *Song*. Most of them were persecuted in their day because they dared to describe the spiritual ecstasies of the union they enjoyed with Christ. In the Middle Ages, Bridal Theology evoked a significant and historic spiritual awakening. It was a revival that swept through the convents and monasteries of Europe. These Christian mystics adopted the language of the *Song* to express their own longing for God. Bernard of Clairvaux, for instance, produced an extensive series of sermons based solely on the holy poem. Saint Ambrose, the fourth century bishop of Milan, preached what he called the ***conubii foedere copulatur,*** in which the soul of man is joined in covenant marriage to Christ. He wrote about Jesus being the Lover of the soul and even told of being awakened from sleep

---

[50] Isaiah 54:5
[51] I Kings 4:32

as he literally felt his mouth being touched by the lips of Jesus. The early Christian scholar, Origen, wrote three entire commentaries on the *Song of Songs.* The *Spiritual Canticle,* written by St. John of the Cross, describes the soul of man as the Bride searching for the Bridegroom.

Women also helped advance the understanding of Solomon's love song. St. Teresa of Avila, a contemporary of St. John of the Cross, wrote the controversial *Concepts of the Love of God,* which she based on the *Song of Songs.* Likewise, the 17th century French mystic,[52] Madame Jeanne Guyon, published a classic commentary on the *Song.* Her books were so controversial they were banned and even burned! Eventually, she was imprisoned eight years for simply claiming to have experienced the love of God as a source of divine, intimate pleasure. In her autobiography, she claims to have been so under the influence of the Holy Spirit as she wrote her commentary on the *Song of Songs,* that she completed the entire task in less than two days!

Interpreting "Experiences"

By citing these early Christian authors and theologians, I do not mean to endorse every word they wrote or validate every experience they describe. In the same way we measure our own experiences through the lens of our particular religious culture and belief system, these ardent Catholic believers interpreted their experiences the only way they could which was within the context of their Catholicism. Seen through that religious framework, the Virgin Mary became both the Mother of God and the Bride of Christ - *a confusing paradox to say the least!* Possibly as an over-reaction to the way the Catholic believers relished Bridal Theology

---

[52] The term "mystic" refers to a Christian who aspires to apprehend spiritual truths by experiential as well as by intellectual means.

church reformer, Martin Luther, sought to marginalize it. As a result, the Protestant church has never really developed a clear understanding of Bridal Theology. *But that is changing today.*

Man Was Not Created in the Garden

Human history began with a love story and a wedding. A careful reading of the biblical account of Creation, however, reveals it did not happen in the way most of us were taught. For instance, man was *not* formed in the Garden of Eden as is generally accepted. The Bible says that Adam was created in *Eden* and then *"put"* into the Garden. That means that Eden and the Garden were two separate places.

> And the LORD God formed man of dust from the ground, and breathed into his nostrils the breath of life; and man became a living being. The LORD God planted a garden eastward in Eden, <u>and there he put the man whom he had formed</u>.[53] [emphasis added]

To be precise, it never was the Garden *of* Eden but the Garden *in* Eden. God created a place called "Eden" and there He planted the Garden. The distinction between where man was *formed* and where he was *placed* is not a minor point. It actually has important meaning as I will show.

Created For Pleasure

The word "Eden" (עדן) means the place of "pleasure." In contrast to this, the Garden was the place prepared for man to

---

[53] Genesis 2:7-8 RSV

work. God was careful not to link the two places. He did not create man *in* the Garden lest he think that the reason he was created was to work and produce something for God. God wanted man to know that the primary reason for his existence was to experience the *pleasure* of being loved by God!

Likewise, you and I were not created in this world. We began our own journey of life in the little "edens" of *our mother's womb.* We were "formed" in that secret place separate and apart from the world. Our very conception was the direct result of *pleasure.* You and I began as a gleam in our father's eye and a sigh on our mother's lips. For nine months or so we enjoyed the rest of just "being." Then, on the day of our birth, we were taken from our "eden" and *placed* into the "garden" of this world. We must never forget, however, that this world is not our place of origin!

What Do You Do?

When two people meet, one of the first questions they ask each other is "What do you do?" We are so far removed from the true reason for our existence that we define each other by what we *do* rather than who we are! Often when men retire from their work, they come face to face with just how meaningless their lives are apart from their work. Not working strips them of their very identity. Some of them become so depressed they take their own lives. What we *do* in life does not define who we are! Our meaning, value, and worth are found in our relationship with God. *We are His Beloved!* Perhaps you have heard it said that Christians are "saved to serve." *I disagree!* I believe we are saved so that we might *love and be loved by God.* If we accept the premise that we were "saved to serve," we doom ourselves to a life of trying to find our value in what we *do* rather than for who we *are.* We will believe our value to God is linked directly to what we can produce for Him. The truth is - you and I already *have* great value to God simply because He has chosen to love us. We were *not* "saved to serve" - *we were saved to know love!*

Adam's Longing for a Bride

We know that Adam was made *in the image of God,* but I believe he was also created to *be an image of God.* Consider how God planned for Adam to live without a companion for a space of time. After observing that all living things possessed suitable mates,[54] he also observed that he had no one. If God's eventual plan was to make mankind as both male and female, why did He not create them both simultaneously? I believe it was because God was "imaging" something through Adam. God wanted Adam to live alone *until* his loneliness gave birth to the desire to have someone to love. At the moment Adam felt the heartache of *not* having someone to love, God's *own* eternal longing for a suitable companion was revealed. Adam's desire for a mate was a visible picture of the same yearning that was present in the heart of Jesus before time began. Thus, the story of Adam and his bride set the stage for the development of the Bridal theme that can be traced through the entire Bible.

A Wedding on Mt. Sinai

When God delivered His Law to Israel at Mt. Sinai, the Rabbis teach that He descended from heaven, kissed the mouth of Israel, and took her as His wife. The thick clouds that clung to the mountain provided the wedding canopy called the "chuppah."[55] Today, nearly every Jewish couple still say their wedding vows beneath a chuppah as a reminder of those awesome clouds that

---

[54] Genesis 2:20

[55] When Jewish couples marry they stand beneath a covering made of fabric that is held by each corner on poles.

clung to Mt. Sinai when God made His covenant with their ancestors.

As Israel's marriage to God developed, problems eventually emerged and so God sought the help of "marriage counselors" called "prophets" to address those problems. When God spoke through His prophets, He spoke tenderly as a husband speaks to his wife. Jeremiah, for instance, generously employs bridal language in his message to Israel. He likens their unfaithfulness, not to rebellion or disobedience, but to adultery.[56] When Israel went after other gods it was said that she "played the harlot."[57] When her adultery finally became too much for Jehovah to bear, He even provided her with a formal "bill of divorcement."[58]

A Divine Romance

Bridal Theology recognizes that at the very heart of the story of redemption lies the story of a divine romance, which is portrayed by the natural husband/wife relationship. Marriage metaphors, allusions to Jewish wedding customs and bridal language permeate the teachings of Jesus. God's covenant with His people has always been, and will always be, much more than a cold legal arrangement. It is the joining of hearts through a marriage covenant.

While the Bible describes the people of God in various terms such as a vine, sheep, and living stones, these are merely metaphors. The Bride of Christ, however, is *not* a metaphor. It is the term that describes the very substance and reality of our true identity. Jesus is not *like* a Bridegroom, He really *is* the Bridegroom. And we are not *like* a bride – we really *are* His Bride.

---

[56] Jeremiah 23:10
[57] Jeremiah 3:1
[58] Jeremiah 3:8

The Marriage of the Lamb, as well, is a real event that will occur at the end of the age. If the Bride is just a metaphor, then Jesus, it seems, will be left standing at the altar!

5

THE SONG OF SONGS

See! The winter is past; the rains are over and gone.
Flowers appear on the earth; the season of singing has come, the cooing of doves is heard in our land.
Song of Songs 2:11-12

The Key to the Lock

In the Middle Ages, a Jewish scholar described the *Song of Songs* as "a lock to which the keys have been lost."[59] While this expresses the enigmatic quality of the *Song*, I have come to believe that the *Song* is not like a lock at all. In fact, it is the *key* which unlocks the great and profound revelations of the Word of God!

Today, there is a resurgence of interest in the study of the *Song of Songs*, and people all over the world are beginning to ponder what it means to be the Bride of Jesus. I believe the next - and perhaps the *last* - great spiritual awakening will grow out of a revelation of Bridal love. *And the Song of Songs is indeed the key that will unlock this powerful awakening.*

A Window of Revelation

The *Song* yields its vast wealth of revelation on so many levels that a revered Rabbi in the first century said, "Had not the

[59] Saadia Ben Joseph

Torah been given, The Song of Solomon would have sufficed to guide the world." [60] That would be quite an achievement for such a little book! The Bible says that the secrets of God's wisdom are *double* what they seem.[61] The word "double" in Hebrew is "kephel" and it means "possessing many layers." I have found that the *Song of Songs* is not just one revelation but multiple layers of revelation which, like the proverbial onion, must be peeled back one by one. It is a story which is literal and symbolic; historic and prophetic. It is germane to the past, present and future all at once. The *Song* is both "nitty-gritty" and down-to-earth while remaining utterly transcendent at the same time. It is simple yet profoundly complex. Historically, it has been viewed as a series of poems telling about the courtship of King Solomon and a young woman called the Shulamite. The book is almost entirely a dialog between these two lovers. *But it is so much more than that, as well.*

Understanding the Mystery: Metaphors

As an example of poetry, the *Song* is unequaled in its lyrical composition and use of vibrant imagery. It engages the reader in beautiful metaphors and brilliant symbolism. In fact, nearly two hundred metaphors are employed in the *Song*, and that is where the real riches of the book are found.

De-coding the meaning of the symbols and metaphors employed in the *Song* is one of the keys to unlocking its secrets. In the 7th chapter of the Song, we find an example of the use of metaphor.

> ...Your eyes [are] like the pools in Heshbon, By the gate of Bath-rab'bim.[62]

---

[60] Rabbi Akiba Ben Joseph
[61] Job 11:6
[62] Song of Songs 7:4b

Here, Solomon extols the beauty of his bride by comparing her eyes with the water pools in Heshbon. In ancient times, Heshbon was an oasis town replete with lush gardens and restful pools. After a long journey, camels were led to Heshbon to drink and rest in the cool shade of the garden. The word "Bath-rabbim," in direct contrast, means "populated city" and brings to mind a busy marketplace. What can be understood from this metaphor? Perhaps one meaning is that those who possess the qualities of the Bride know how to draw apart from the clamor and distractions of life to commune with the Bridegroom in the quiet oasis of personal prayer and worship.

Understanding the Mystery: Allegory

Much of the intrigue of the *Song* also lies in the fact that it was written to be an allegory and is therefore a story with two meanings, one literal and the other symbolic. Allegorical story-telling uses objects, persons, and actions within the story as personifications of other objects, persons, and actions that exist *outside* of the narrative itself. The *Song* uses the marriage union as an allegory to illustrate the relationship of God with His people. As we read about the physical love-making of Solomon and the Shulamite, it becomes a window of revelation into the kind of intimate relationship Christ yearns to share with His own spiritual Bride. Think of the *Song* as a drama in which the actors actually represent other real people or things. To understand what the book is about, therefore, it is necessary to define the characters in the book.

My own interpretation of the main characters is as follows:

- Solomon represents Jesus, the Bridegroom.
- The Shulamite is the Bride of Jesus.

- The Shulamite's brothers are the voice of Religion.
- The Daughters of Jerusalem are believers who are distinct from the Bride.
- The Watchmen represent spiritual authorities.

If you keep this "cast of characters" in mind as you read the story, the deeper meaning of the story will begin to unfold.

A Book Out Of Place

Some scholars, rejecting the allegorical interpretation of the book, have questioned the *Song's* legitimate right to even be included in the Canon of Scripture at all! They think it lacks theological depth and content. *Nothing could be further from the truth!* Some even suggest that it should have been considered an extra-biblical writing. Admittedly, the *Song* does seem strangely out of place among the other great books of the Bible, and on the surface it does seem to lack theological substance. The name of God, for instance, is found only once in the entire book, and even then it is an obscure inclusion.[63] Christian theologians have long debated whether the book should be understood simply as a love song written by Solomon or something deeper. *Personally, I think it is both.* Certainly the concept of God as a husband is not a new one. An Old Testament prophet said "Your Maker is your husband,"[64] and in the book of Ephesians, Paul clearly advanced the idea that the marriage between a man and a woman does indeed serve as a living metaphor for the love relationship between Christ and His Church. He calls this mystical, spiritual union between God and man a "deep and profound mystery."[65]

[63] Song of Songs 8:6 The Hebrew name "Jah" is found in this verse and is a term which means "God." See Young's Literal Translation of the Bible.
[64] Isaiah 54:5
[65] See Ephesians 5:31-32

Unfortunately, however, the *Song* is too often presented as nothing more than a sort of marriage manual for how to build and maintain a happy home. Certainly it *can* be interpreted at that level, but the true, hidden riches await those who penetrate beyond the superficial veneer of the story to explore its many beautiful layers.

The Council at Jamnia

In the first century, Jewish teachers of the Law met at what is called the Council of Jamnia. They gathered to decide what writings would be canonized as sacred Jewish text. The *Song of Songs* was a book in hot dispute. Most of the teachers considered it to be a mere collection of wedding poems with uncertain meaning. One of the scholars, named Rabbi Akiba ben Joseph, however, proved persuasive in arguing in favor of the inclusion of the book. Concerning its importance, he wrote:

> "No one in Israel disputes that the Song of Songs is a divine book. All the world is not worth the day on which the Song of Songs was given to Israel, for all the Writings are holy, but the Song of Songs is the Holy of Holies." [66]

By likening the *Song of Songs* to the Holy of Holies, Rabbi Akiba attributed the most supreme quality to the book. To say that it *exceeded* the importance of even the Law makes it not only the greatest love poem ever written but also the greatest revelation given to man by God! Indeed, today it is not even possible to think of Jewish spirituality without including the *Song of Songs,* since

---

[66]Mishnah Yadayim 3:5

both the Midrash[67] and the Targum[68] venerate it as the greatest expression of God's love for Israel.

Solomon's Trilogy

Although we tend to view the three books of Solomon as stand-alone books, many of the ancients considered them an important trilogy which spoke of three different types of wisdom made available by God to man: those being *natural wisdom, experiential wisdom* and *wisdom of intimate knowing.* They saw a parallel of the three books and the three compartments of the Temple. Proverbs was thought to be the book of *natural wisdom,* synonymous with the Temple's Outer Court which was illuminated by the *natural light* of the sun. Today, we often refer to this kind of wisdom as "common sense." Proverbs is really a book of *probabilities* rather than promises. It lays out what we might call the "cause and effect" of life. If we act in a certain way, we should expect a certain outcome.

Ecclesiastes, on the other hand, speaks of the kind of wisdom that comes by actually *experiencing* life. It is a deep inquiry into the meaning of life itself. All through the book of Ecclesiastes, Solomon searches for deeper meaning to life's questions by engaging in every experience life has to offer. We might call this kind of wisdom "street smarts" or "the school of hard knocks." Ultimately, Solomon came to the conclusion that life is empty without God. The Jews equated Ecclesiastes to that part of the Temple called the Holy Place. In that interior room, a lamp called a menorah was used to illuminate the room. Light which was kindled and maintained by human means, as contrasted to

---

[67] Rabbinical work with homiletic interpretations

[68] An Aramaic translation of the Hebrew Bible (Tanoak) compiled from the Second Temple period until the middle Ages.

the natural light of the sun, is an appropriate symbol for the seeking heart of man since it requires man's effort.

The final book in the trilogy, the *Song of Songs*, beckons man to seek the deepest kind of wisdom there is - that which comes from *intimate knowing*. This form of wisdom, as Rabbi Akiba pointed out, is synonymous with the Holiest of Holies. The only source of light that shone in that inner chamber was the *shekinah*[69] light which emanated from the very presence of God Himself!

Abraham, Isaac, Jacob

The lives of the three Patriarchs also represent the three kinds of wisdom. Abraham represents the spiritual life lived in the natural wisdom of simple faith and obedience.[70] There are many Christians today who live this way by putting the highest premium on believing and adhering to right doctrine.

Isaac, on the other hand, was a "digger of wells."[71] He symbolizes the kind of believer who goes beyond simple faith and obedience to dig deeper into the meaning of life. This kind of believer knows that true spirituality is more than just rule-keeping.

Jacob, who represents the *wisdom of intimate knowing*, drew even closer to the Divine; close enough to actually see and touch God! His eyes were opened to see the angels of God ascending and descending between heaven and earth. His vision was actually a theophany of Jesus![72] He represents those who have

---

[69] Shekinah is a Hebrew word which represents God's outshining presence.
[70] Genesis 12:1-4
[71] Genesis 26:18
[72] A theophany is an appearance of Jesus Christ to people before His birth. (See John 1:51 where Jesus identified Himself with the vision Jacob had)

entered into a more personal, intimate relationship with God[73] and who see and experience things that others will never see nor experience.

Shulamites Arising

Often, when I am teaching a large group of people, I will ask them to raise their hands if they know that God loves them. Without fail, almost everyone in the room raises their hand. This is not surprising since, as a point of theology, we all know that God loves us. However, when asked to raise their hands if they actually *feel loved* by God - usually only a few hands can be seen across the room. I truly sense that many believers long for something *more* than what they are presently experiencing. With all the sophisticated, well-executed programs the Church can offer people today, there remains a deep hunger for intimacy and relationship in our hearts.

Chasing After the Anointing

In the beginning verses of the *Song*, the Bride says:

> Let him kiss me with the kisses of his mouth: for Your love is better than wine. Because of the fragrance of your good ointments, Your name is ointment poured forth, Therefore do the virgins love You.[74]

Here we find one of the many plays-on-words which exist in the *Song*. The Hebrew word translated "name" is *shem* (שם). The word for "ointment" is *shemen* (שמן). Both words look and sound much

[73] Genesis 32:24
[74] Song of Songs 1:2-3

the same. Shemen describes the sacred oil of the Temple used in the consecration of kings and priests. Jesus has been given the "name" (shem) "that is above every name"[75] and His name carries the anointing (shemen) of God.

But as desirable as the king's anointing was, the Shulamite wanted something more. Her deepest desire was to possess the king's *name* as her own. While the young and immature girls (alma המלע) were infatuated with the "anointing" of Solomon, the Shulamite wanted nothing less than the "kisses of his mouth."

Many today chase frantically after the anointing, yet they fail to build an authentic devotional life of intimacy with Christ. While it seems that much of the Church is infatuated with the *power of God,* a smaller number are discovering the superior reward that comes to those who value and seek the *Presence of God.* They are the "Shulamites" who yearn for a real relationship *with* God more than just obtaining a blessing *from* God. They have tasted something so real and rewarding that it transcends lesser things.

[75] Philippians 2:10

6

THE EROS OF GOD

A sex symbol becomes a thing. I hate being a thing.
Marilyn Monroe

Erotic Literature

Would you be shocked to learn that Bible scholars classify the *Song of Songs* as the *erotic* literature of the Bible? If you have already dared to venture into the book, you know that it is frank indeed in its depiction of the pleasures of human sexuality. We need to be reminded that true eroticism is neither vulgar nor profane. While popular culture links even the vilest forms of pornography with eroticism, pornography is actually the polar opposite of true eroticism. Pope John Paul II wrote, "the problem with pornography is not that it shows *too much* of a woman, but that it shows *too little.*" By that, he meant that pornography fails to portray people as God created them, crowned with the dignity of the *Imago Dei.*[76] Sex ceases to be a vital expression of our personhood when it is reduced to a biological function or a commercialized commodity. Thus the way we value our sexuality is the way we value ourselves.

Our sexuality is a real paradox. It can either be something

---

[76] Latin for "image of God."

so degraded and obscene that it robs us of our human dignity, or it can be something so transcendently beautiful it demands to be celebrated in poetry and art; *even the poetry of the Bible!* In the *Song,* God blesses human love, romance and even erotic pleasure with a shameless kind of glory that is breath-taking to some but also disconcerting to those who cannot relish the idea that sex possesses a spiritual dimension.

Paradise Restored

Solomon treats the sensual nature of erotic love with artistic delicacy by expertly cloaking many of the more intimate scenes of the *Song* in poetic metaphor. Nevertheless, the amorous tone of the book still makes it an unusual and intriguing addition to the biblical library. To Solomon's credit, the eroticism of the book is never crude or provocative. Instead, the holy mystery is concealed within the beautiful imagery of things found in nature. The image of a garden, for instance, is used extensively in the poem as a representation of the Shulamite's body. In one place, Solomon calls her his "garden enclosed."[77] It is a phrase which extols her moral chastity. Solomon also describes their lovemaking by comparing himself to an apple tree[78] standing in the grove. He depicts her as reclining beneath him as she "tastes his pleasant fruit."[79] To the discerning person, the sexual meaning is clear. Solomon's writing style shifts the emphasis away from the physical act of lovemaking and helps the reader focus on the deeper qualities of romance and intimacy instead. The garden motif is also a likely allusion to the fact that the union between God and man was originally *lost* in a garden. The word Solomon uses to describe his bride is the Hebrew word "*gan.*" It is the same

---

[77] Song of Songs 4:12
[78] Song of Songs 2:3
[79] Song of Songs 2:3

word used to describe the original Garden (gan) of Eden. The meaning could not be clearer: *The love that is shared between Christ and His Bride is the restoration of the Paradise that was lost between God and man in the original Garden.*

Sexuality and Spirituality

When our relationship with Christ is viewed as a marriage, it necessitates our facing the issue of how our sexuality relates to our spirituality. Unfortunately, much of the church has developed an unbiblical, distorted view of human sexuality. We often think of our sexuality as being the "lower part" of our personhood and our spirituality as the "higher part." The Bible, however, teaches no such thing. We use terms such as being "in the flesh" to indicate that we are motivated by our lower carnal passions as opposed to "being in the Spirit" which denotes that we are following the higher, more noble path. The separation of flesh from spirit is opposed to Jewish doctrine concerning the nature of man and in fact is the seedbed for the heresy of Gnosticism.[80] In Judaism, the flesh of man is just as sacred as his soul and the expression of love and intimacy between a man and his wife is considered the highest expression of one's spirituality! In mainstream Christian thought, unfortunately, sexuality is often viewed merely as a troublesome sin-related problem. Since we are created in the image of God with all the characteristics of God's person and personality, does it not make reasonable sense to imagine that God feels something akin to the same kind of passion that drives us to seek intimate oneness with another person? I think the problem we sometimes have with imagining Jesus as a passionate, romantic Bridegroom says more about our own

---

[80] Gnostic teachers taught that the flesh was evil and the spirit divine. Therefore, Jesus could not have come literally in the flesh. This error infiltrated the early church and was combated strongly by the Apostle John.

unresolved issues and fears regarding intimacy and sexuality than about anything else. According to Bridal Theology, the reason God seeks, saves, and restores fallen humanity is not solely to take us to heaven. He has saved us so that we might experience the affectionate joy of His love and ultimately be presented to Jesus Christ at the end of the age as His glorious Bride. *The end result of our redemption is our enjoyment of God and His enjoyment of us.*

Controversy

In A. R. Faussett's commentary on the *Song of Songs,* he points out that in ancient times it was forbidden for anyone to even study the *Song* before the age of thirty precisely because of its bold sensual language.[81] To avoid controversy, many commentators have sought to soften the erotic content of the book by either draping it in shallow sentimentality or by applying an interpretation based in hyper-spiritualization. However, the *Song* itself does not treat human sexuality with such prudish suppression. Sex, in the *Song,* is presented solely for the sake of joy, relationship, and pleasure! Surprisingly, it extols sexual union completely apart from the expectation of producing progeny! This seems to be incongruous to the ancient patriarchal culture where women were valued almost solely for their ability to produce children. This is not the case, however, for the woman in the *Song*. She is desired, not for what she can produce, but simply because her King "greatly desires [her] beauty."[82] This is one of the most important messages of the book: *that we have value and worth to God apart from what we will ever do for Him; and that He derives great pleasure simply by loving us.*

[81] Commentary Critical and Explanatory on the Whole Bible, by A.R. Fausset
[82] Psalm 45:11 Author's paraphrase

Soul-Bonding

The Bible often describes the sexual union between a man and a woman by using the phrase "he went in unto her."[83] Bluntly speaking, this is not simply referring to the physical act of coitus. It is much deeper than that. It means that the very *soul* of the man *entered into* the soul of the woman as they made love. This bonding of two souls is considered so important to marriage that Jewish men were forbidden by religious law to work or go to war for a full year after they married! A husband's sole purpose in life for the first year of marriage was to "cheer up his wife."[84] This same soul-bonding occurs every time we give ourselves sexually to another person, whether married to them or not. Through acts of intimacy, we open the door of our souls and invite others to delve into the spiritual essence of who we are. In so doing, we give away a little part of our soul to our partner and take a little part of their soul into us as well. This is the reason God has called us to sexual purity and fidelity in marriage and has so strongly warned us to "flee immorality."[85] He knows that sexual soul-bonding with *one* mate in the context of marriage ultimately gives us a positive sense of significance and wholeness. But He also knows that *promiscuity does just the opposite.* Unbridled sexual experiences lead to the fragmenting of our souls as we give ourselves away to people with whom we have no long-term *covenant connection.*

Personality Disorders

Many personality disorders, such as Dissociative Identity

---

[83] See Genesis 16:2
[84] Deuteronomy 24:5 KJV
[85] 1 Corinthians 6:18 KJV

Disorder (also known as Multiple Personality Disorder), have been linked directly to sexual promiscuity and childhood sexual abuse. In the context of a long-term marriage commitment, soul-bonding through sexual intimacy is a good thing because it enables a couple to grow together in unity. In short-term commitments outside of marriage or in the case of sexual abuse, soul-bonding can prove disastrous!

Commonly, when pre-marital sexual relationships fall apart (as they usually do), it is not long before another sexual partner is acquired and the soul-bonding continues - *only with a different person.* With each successive sex partner, the soul becomes even more diffused. People who have led sexually promiscuous lifestyles often experience severe emotional brokenness and confusion later in life. God's perfect design is for two souls to become one soul in marriage. When we go beyond what God has prescribed, it can lead to mental and emotional torment.

Looking at this strictly from a biological perspective, if a person in their lifetime has an average of eight sex partners, they will have had indirect sexual exposure to almost three million people! When we have intercourse with one person, we are, in effect, having intercourse with all of their previous partners. As frightening as this is, when you consider the compounded spiritual "DNA" that is also passed between intimate partners, it is no wonder that the need for deliverance and inner healing is so great in the Body of Christ.

Satan Has Targeted Our Sexuality

When the Apostle Paul wrote to the church at Ephesus about the profound mystery of a couple becoming one flesh through marriage, he was really speaking of something even more profound: *the spiritual union of Christ with His Bride!*[86] The marriage union is used as a metaphor of this deep spiritual mystery no less than fourteen times in the New Testament! Since the expression of love through sexual intimacy in marriage is a living metaphor which serves to illustrate the quality of Christ's love for His Bride, it is no wonder that Satan has chosen our sexuality as his primary target. Satan seeks to destroy God's blueprint for holy love, passion and intimacy so we will become estranged not only from God, *but from each other as well.*

---

[86] See Ephesians 5:31-32

7

THE BRIDEGROOM

As the bridegroom rejoices over the bride,
so shall your God rejoice over you.
Isaiah 62:5

The True Nature of God

Although in times past, God appeared to certain men and women in various forms, He never *fully* revealed Himself to anyone. Moses came close when he witnessed God's vague receding glory,[87] but even then he did not have a full vision of the Holy One. When Jesus appeared, however, the Bible teaches that He was an exact representation of God.[88] In what role, then, did Jesus come? Each of the four Gospels presents Him clearly as the *Bridegroom!* Through the Incarnation, Jesus pulled back the curtain to let mankind see the *true* nature of God which had been shrouded in mystery until then. Who is God? *He is our Husband, our Lover, and our Bridegroom!*

Insight into the Revelation

---

[87] Exodus 33:23 The implication is not that Moses saw God's back, but that God kept a safe distance so as not to kill him.
[88] Hebrews 1:3

A thousand years before Christ came, Solomon ruled as King of Israel. His reign lasted forty years, and during that time, he built the nation into a vast and powerful kingdom rivaling the greatest empires of the world. So great was His kingdom, he did not even bother to take an inventory of the silver vessels in his treasury because of the over-abundance of gold! His stables alone housed a staggering number of 12,000 horses and 1,400 chariots![89]

Although he was a young king, Solomon's wisdom and mental prowess became legendary. Tradition says that once a year he hosted a sort of "mental Olympics" where the wisest sages would convene to challenge him with riddles and conundrums. It is possible that the Queen of Sheba made her famous pilgrimage to Jerusalem to attend one of those annual events.[90]

Since Solomon serves as a figure of Christ, a study of his life gives insight into Jesus Christ and His kingdom. During Solomon's reign, for example, Israel ascended to the zenith of her glory, as will the reign of Christ during His future millennial kingdom. Indeed, Jesus even spoke of the superiority of His coming dynasty to that of Solomon's when He said:

> The Queen of the south will rise up in the judgment with this generation and condemn it for she came from the ends of the earth to hear the wisdom of Solomon; and, indeed, a ***greater than Solomon is here.***[91] [emphasis added]

Solomon's Two Names

David named his son "Solomon" which means "peace." At the time of his birth, Bathsheba was still grieving the death of their first son. Perhaps David chose this name hoping the birth of

---

[89] 1 Kings 4:26
[90] 1 Kings 10:1
[91] Matthew 12:42

another child would console his wife.[92] Later, the prophet Nathan gave Solomon a *second* name. It was the prophetically significant name, Jedidiah,[93] which means *"The Beloved."* In the *Song*, Solomon almost always refers to himself by this unique prophetic name, indicating that the *Song* has a prophetic meaning.

Jesus as the Beloved

Many today find little significance to the *Song of Songs.* However, if we had been Jews living during the time of Christ, our estimation of the book would have been much different. They saw the book as a prophetic promise upon which they hung their hopes. It told of the Messiah who would appear one day in the persona of the *"Beloved,"* of whom Solomon was a type. This expectation was so well entrenched in Jewish belief that the term *"Beloved"* was commonly used as a Messianic title. Nearly 800 years before Jesus appeared, the prophet Hosea promised that God would return, cleanse unfaithful Israel from her spiritual adultery, and restore her to her wedding vows.

> Therefore I am now going to allure her; I will lead her into the desert and speak tenderly to her. There I will give her back her vineyards, and will make the Valley of Achor a door of hope. ..."In that day," declares the Lord, "you will call me 'my husband'; you will no longer call me 'my master.' ...[and] *I will betroth you to me forever..."*[94] [emphasis added]

With this earnest expectation in the air, Jesus appeared as the Bridegroom of Israel! When He was baptized by his cousin

---

[92] 2 Samuel 12
[93] 2 Samuel 12:25
[94] Hosea 2:14,19 RSV

John, it is recorded that the Father spoke from heaven and said,

> This is my *beloved* Son, in whom I am well pleased.[95]

In *Young's Literal Translation* of the Bible, this verse is more accurately translated from the original language as,

> This is My Son -- **the Beloved**, in whom I did delight.[96]

This more precise rendering reveals that the word *"Beloved"* is a proper title rather than a descriptive word. The Father plainly identified Jesus as the literal embodiment of the *Beloved Bridegroom* for Whom the Jews sorely pined. In essence the Father's declaration that day was,

> This is my Son, and He is *your* Bridegroom![97]

Further evidence that the Jews expected Messiah to appear as their Bridegroom can be seen in the way John the Baptist answered those who asked if he might be the Messiah. John could have answered plainly by saying, "I am not Messiah" but instead, he chose to say,

> I am not the Christ but am sent ahead of him. ***The bride belongs to the bridegroom.*** The friend who attends the bridegroom waits and listens for him, and is full of joy when he hears the bridegroom's voice. [98] [emphasis added]

---

[95] Matthew 3:17

[96] Robert Young, The Holy Bible, Consisting of the Old and New Covenants; Translated according to the Letter and Idioms of the Original Languages. Edinburgh: George Adam Young & Co., 1863.

[97] Author's paraphrase

[98] John 3:28-29 RSV

It is clear by John's answer that he knew they were expecting the Messiah to come in the role of their Bridegroom, so he answered them accordingly.

The True Identity of Jesus

From the moment Jesus stepped out of the waters of the Jordan, His thoughts and actions were clearly those of the Bridegroom. His first miracle, for instance, was performed at a wedding in Cana of Galilee. When teaching, He often illustrated His stories by talking about weddings and by using wedding imagery to describe the nature of the Kingdom of God. I think He did so because He wanted us to understand that everything is really about *one thing* - our own future wedding!

When the Apostle Paul wrote to the church he had founded at Corinth, he reminded them that he had betrothed them to Christ in order to present them as a pure bride to one husband.[99] He also expressed his deep concern that they were being led away from knowing and experiencing Christ as their Bridegroom. To this end, he wrote:

> …if someone comes and preaches *another Jesus* than the one we preached, or if you receive a different spirit from the one you received, or if you accept a different gospel from the one you accepted, you submit to it readily enough.[100] [emphasis added]

From this, it is clear that the "Jesus" Paul preached to the Corinthian believers was their Bridegroom. The *spirit* they received was that of their own identity as His Bride. He warned them against accepting any concept of Jesus other than the one

---

[99] 2 Corinthians 11:2 Author's paraphrase of RSV
[100] 2 Corinthians 11:4 RSV

which he had first presented to them - *that of their Bridegroom!* It is important to see that when we conceive of Christ in any identity other than that of our Bridegroom, it results in our receiving what Paul calls "another spirit." The spirit of the Bride cannot live in us if we do not recognize and receive Christ as our Bridegroom.

The Eternal Bridegroom

I find it interesting that Jesus is exclusively called the "Bridegroom" and never the "Husband." There are less than seven thousand words in the Hebrew language compared with about one million in the English language.[101] Since there are fewer words to choose from, the choice of certain words is highly significant. Jesus is called the Bridegroom because that word connotes a love that is fresh, exciting, and passionate. We might call it the experience of "first love." You will recall that when Jesus addressed the church at Ephesus in the book of Revelation, He exhorted them to rekindle the fire of their "first love" experience. He, on the other hand, never has to return to His first love *because He never leaves it!* His love for us will never cool or grow so familiar it loses its passion. A million years from now, His love for us will still burn with the same desire He feels for us today. *A million years from now He will still be our Bridegroom!*

The Many Wives of Solomon

Solomon married many wives. The *Song,* however, is the account of his betrothal to only one of those wives. She was the one and only woman who would ever truly own his heart. There are those who contend that Solomon cannot possibly serve as a

---

[101] Easton's Bible Dictionary, Easton, Matthew George (1823-1894)

type of Christ since he had 700 wives and 300 concubines.[102] It is certainly true that his foreign wives eventually turned Solomon's heart to idolatry, but if this disqualifies him as a type of Christ, then neither is David a suitable type since he was both an adulterer and a murderer! Those in the Bible who serve as *types* of Christ are just that - *mere types.* Their lives are understandably imperfect representations of the perfect Christ. Ironically, the fact that Solomon had many wives actually makes him a *more* accurate type of Christ as we will see!

Treaty Wives

Many of the women Solomon married were called "treaty wives." He married them as an act of political expediency in order to secure peace with neighboring kingdoms. Although the male ego is admittedly large, no man possesses the prowess to maintain a harem of a thousand women! It is probable that Solomon never even saw many of his treaty wives after their wedding day. By virtue of the union, they became queens and enjoyed all the privileges associated with that royal position. They had everything a queen should have *except* a real and intimate relationship with the King. Unfortunately, this closely describes the relationship many believers have with Christ today. They have accepted His covenant and secured their place in His kingdom. They enjoy all the blessings that come by virtue of that fact. In essence, they live like queens! What they do not have is an intimate relationship with their King. Christ, like Solomon, does indeed have many "treaty wives." This sad reality is explained in the *Song of Songs:*

There are sixty queens and eighty concubines, and

[102] 1 Kings 11:3

> maidens without number. My dove, my perfect one, is only one...[103] [emphasis added]

Even though Solomon was bound by covenant to many wives, only one truly possessed his heart. *That is the honor reserved for the Bride of Christ.*

[103] Song of Songs 6:8-9 RSV

8

THE BRIDE

It is not good that man should live alone;
I will make him a help mate.
Book of Genesis

A Life with a Purpose

Everyone had their own expectations for Jesus, but He refused to live any kind of life other than the one that had been planned for Him by His Father. He came as the eternal Bridegroom and to live any other way would have been fraudulent. How about you? Are you living out the authentic script written for you by God or have you opted for something less? You were created to become the Bride of Christ! Are you living your true identity?

The Little Lost Coin

Jesus once told a story about a woman who had ten coins and misplaced one.[104] She lit a lamp and searched every nook and cranny of her house until she found it. Then she planned a party and called her friends and neighbors together to celebrate the finding of that one little coin. The total value of the coin was insignificant. The story seems absurd since the celebration party

---

[104] Luke 15:8

alone cost many times more than what the coin was worth. The key to understanding how one little coin could be so valuable is found in the ancient Jewish customs. When a woman married, her friends often took coins, punched holes in them, strung them together and fashioned them into a beautiful head-band which she wore on her wedding day. Losing one of those coins was tantamount to losing one's wedding ring today! Likewise, even though we are not always aware of our own significance to God, we possess a worth that is "far above rubies."[105] To Jesus, His Bride is nothing less than His reward for going to the Cross!

Milk and Honey

In *Song of Songs* 4:11, Solomon speaks to his bride:

> Your lips distil nectar, my bride; **honey and milk** are under your tongue; the scent of your garments is like the scent of Lebanon. (RSV) [emphasis added]

The phrase "milk and honey" is one that every Jew knows well. When Moses was describing the Jew's land of promise, he called it a "land flowing with milk and honey."[106] Over time, this phrase came to mean the blessing of Jehovah and the physical land of inheritance. Even a man's own little plot of land was called his personal "milk and honey." Here, however, the "milk and honey" is used as a poetic reference to deep, intimate kissing. In the same way that our inheritance is found in God, His *own* inheritance is found in us! When we allow Him to touch the most intimate areas of our hearts, He considers that *His* milk and honey!

---

[105] Proverbs 31:10
[106] Deuteronomy 27:3

Who is the Bride?

Exactly who comprises the *Beloved* is a subject of strong debate within the church. Some argue that Israel holds that position, while others contend that the church has that unique honor. One thing is made clear in the parable Jesus told of the ten bridal virgins. In that story, He taught that not all who consider themselves a part of the Bridal Company will be taken into the Bridal chamber. The foolish virgins, upon finding the door to the wedding chamber closed, began to cry out for the Lord to grant them entrance only to be told, *"I know you not."* [107]

When John the Baptist was asked *who* the Bridegroom was, he said the Bridegroom was the "one who [had] the bride."[108] Thus, it stands to reason that the Bride is comprised of those who *have* [who know and experience] Christ as their Bridegroom. *It is all about relationship!*

The Church and the Bride

The predominant belief among most major Church denominations is that there is no distinction between the Church and the Bride. They are considered to be synonymous, interchangeable terms. I believe, however, that while the Bride is certainly a *part* of the Church, *the whole Church is not part of the Bride.*

In the New Testament, the Church is called the "Body of Christ." As previously shown, Adam was created - not only in the image of God - but he was also created to *be an image* of God. The *physical* body of Adam, therefore, represents the *spiritual* body of Christ, which is His Church.

---

[107] Matthew 25:12 KJV
[108] John 3:29 KJV

With this in mind, consider the manner in which the first woman (bride) was created. Adam was placed into a deep sleep. God pierced his side and removed a rib. From the opening in Adam's side, blood spilled to the ground. It was the price he would pay to have his bride. Afterward, God brought him back from the deep sleep and presented the woman to him as his companion. Clearly, this is the *image* of which Jesus became the *reality.*

On the Cross, Jesus followed the pattern set by Adam. He too entered into the "deep sleep" *of physical death.* Then a Roman soldier thrust his spear into His *ribcage!* From that wound, blood spilled to the ground. His own shed blood was the price Christ paid for His Bride!

When Adam awoke, he saw his bride as they stood together in the Garden of Eden. When Christ rose from the dead, the first person He saw was also a woman! Mary Magdalene was the first person seen by the risen Lord and this occurred as they stood together in a garden as well! The Bible says that Mary "supposed Him [Jesus] to be the *gardener.*" [109] Thus, Mary serves as one of the archetypes of the eternal Bride.

Consider the fact that the first bride was not the *whole* body of Adam. She was only a small part of him - a rib to be exact. In the same way, the end-time Bride of Christ will be a small remnant (rib) of people who exist within the whole "body of Christ." The moment will arrive, however, when God will bring her out of the Body of Christ and form her into something distinctly different *from* the Church.

All in the Family

In Genesis chapter 24, we read that Abraham sent his trusted servant on a mission to find a bride for his son, Isaac. He

[109] John 20:15 KJV

charged him with these words:

> ...you will <u>not</u> take a wife for my son from the daughters of the Canaanites, among whom I dwell; but you shall go to *my country* and *to my family,* and take a wife for my son.[110] [emphasis added]

Notice that it was from among Abraham's *own people* that Rebecca was called. Jesus sent his disciples into the *whole world* to preach the message of salvation to everyone. The Church is drawn from among all nations. But the Bride is called out from among *God's own people* - the Church! The calling to *Become the Beloved* is not a call to be saved. It is a call *to the saved* to become something *more than saved*. It is the call to be married to God!

To more fully understand our calling and identity as the *spiritual* Bride of Christ, we must dig even deeper into the identity of the bride of King Solomon.

Who Was Solomon's Bride?

The story of Solomon's bride is actually told in two different stories in two different books of the Bible. The first story is of a woman named *Abishag,* found in the book of I Kings. The second story is about a woman called the *Shulamite* in the *Song of Songs*. By comparing the lives of these two women, it becomes obvious that they are actually the same person!

Abishag's Story

During the final days of the life of King David, Abishag served as his personal nurse. In his advanced age, David was no

---

[110] Genesis 24:3-4 NKJV

longer able to retain his body heat. To remedy this, his counselors came up with a rather unique plan. They held a beauty contest and selected a young virgin to sleep with David to keep him warm! Before being selected to serve David, Abishag lived an obscure life working in the vineyards of Shunem. When we compare the first chapter of I Kings with the first chapter of the *Song of Songs* we find that the Shulamite's story perfectly parallels that of Abishag. She too lived an obscure life as a vine-keeper who advanced from working in the fields to serving the King. In the *Song of Songs* we read:

> The king [David] has brought me into his chambers.[111]

Once in the employ of the palace, Abishag (Shulamite) served David night and day. Over time, a special kind of camaraderie developed between them.[112] Their relationship was marked by a deep and affectionate love; nevertheless, she remained a virgin the entire time she served him.

> The young woman was very lovely and she cared for the king, and served him, but the king did not know [cohabit] her.[113] [emphasis added]

Abishag: The Pure Lily

It is difficult to imagine such an arrangement remaining pure in every sense of the word especially when we consider that Abishag was chosen specifically because of her exceptional beauty. We can only imagine that David found her tempting and desirable. The Bible provides a plausible reason for why David

---

[111] Song of Songs 1:4b
[112] 1 Kings 1:4a
[113] 1 Kings 1:4

may have been careful to protect the girl's virginity, and that explanation is found in Psalm 45. Many Bible scholars believe that Psalm 45 is a prophetic vision that David had concerning the wedding of Solomon. Since Solomon is a figure of Christ, it is also viewed as a Messianic vision of the future wedding of Christ and His Bride at the end of time. In the Psalm, David describes seeing his future daughter-in-law standing by Solomon's side on their wedding day. By virtue of the vision given to him, David knew the identity of the Shulamite before she was ever brought to his chamber! His special devotion to maintaining her moral purity was rooted in the foreknowledge that God had already chosen her to be the wife of his son.

Another clue that supports the idea that David knew the identity of the Shulamite before he ever met her is found in the *superscription* of Psalm 45. David dedicated the Psalm to someone he identified mysteriously as the "Shoshannim" (שׁושׁן). Shoshannim is a Hebrew word which means "the lily." In the second chapter of the *Song*, the exact same word is used by the Shulamite when she refers to herself as a *lily!*

> I am the rose of Sharon, and a ***lily*** (lit. Shoshannim) of the valleys.[114] [emphasis added]

Amazingly, David dedicated the prophecy of Psalm 45 to his son's future wife while she was yet unknown to him!

Abishag: The Orphan

Another commonality shared by Abishag and the Shulamite supporting the idea that they were the same person is that they were both *fatherless.* Abishag's name literally means "without father," and other clues found in the *Song* lead us to

---

[114] Song of Songs 2:1 KJV

believe that the Shulamite was fatherless as well. She says, for instance, that it was her *brothers*, not her father, who acted as her caretakers.[115] In the patriarchal life of the ancient Jews, everything related to the father and the father's house. For her brothers to act in her father's stead would indicate that her father was either dead or absent. Also, when speaking of her home life, she refers to her mother but never her father. She even uses the phrase "my mother's house,"[116] indicating matriarchal rule in the home.

My Sister, My Spouse

Knowing that she was destined to become his son's bride, David may well have treated Abishag like his own daughter. Having never known her father, she would have gravitated to the protective love and pure affection he gave her. It's easy to imagine that when Solomon visited his father's bedchamber he would have witnessed firsthand the fatherly affection David showed his nurse. As the king and his son spoke of things pertaining to the kingdom, Abishag probably listened to their conversations as she lay quietly next to David. This may have been the inspiration for what Solomon wrote in the book of Ecclesiastes,

> …if two lie down together, they will keep warm, but how can one be warm alone?[117]

Perhaps it was during those many conversations between father and son that Abishag began to dream about what it might be like to be married to Solomon. Four times in the *Song of Songs,* Solomon uses a special term of endearment for the Shulamite,

---

[115] Song of Songs 8:8-9
[116] Song of Songs 3:4, 8:2
[117] Ecclesiastes 4:11

calling her "my sister, my spouse." Of course she wasn't actually his sister, but because of the unique surrogate father/daughter relationship she shared with David, she was indeed *like* a sister to him before she became his spouse.

Fatherly Love

The level of intimacy that developed between David and Abishag provides a beautiful picture of intimate love that is free from the fear of trespass or transgression. Night after night the girl would lie as close to the king as she desired without fearing that her pure devotion to him would ever be exploited. I believe God has given us this part of the story of Abishag for a very important reason. She represents the orphaned spirit of all mankind. We are all born into the world "without Father." Until we are born *again* by the Spirit of God, we are all spiritual orphans cut off from our true identity. *We don't know who we are because we don't know to Whom we belong.* As we seek to understand more about the nature of Bridal love, we are first told the story of an orphan girl finding the father she never knew. Before any of us are ready to know the intimate, romantic love of our Bridegroom God, we first need to experience the foundational, safe, and unconditional love of our *Father God.*

Love Begins At Home

Ideally, our first experience of intimate love is the experience of family love. The love of our father and mother is the most intimate kind of love we will ever know outside of a sexually intimate relationship. The love we receive from our families, while deeply intimate, is meant to be separate and apart from our sexuality. This non-sexual, unconditional love is the very foundation that prepares us to one day experience healthy, erotic love with our marriage partner. Sadly, however, many children today have become victims of abuse, neglect, or sexual crimes. As adults, they carry within themselves a unique brokenness that stems from the horror of their childhoods. Someone has said that the greatest loss a child experiences when sexually abused by their father is the loss of their father. At the moment the abuse occurs, the child becomes "fatherless," in the sense that he or she can never trust their father again. Chances are that you, the reader, may have been a victim of such abuse and loss. For you, the words "intimacy" and "father" are incongruous and carry a negative connotation. For you, it may seem impossible to imagine that Father God would invite you into His bed just to keep Him warm by your closeness and love. *But, it's true!* In the same way David "did not cohabit with Abishag," your heavenly Father will never hurt you or betray your need to know His intimate love. The Father's bed is a safe bed. In fact, there is healing in His bed!

Healing in the Father's Bed

Often, victims of childhood sexual abuse have difficulty establishing healthy romantic relationships as adults because they have never resolved the pain and brokenness associated with their past abuse. Also we have seen that many people, whether victims of abuse or not, often find it challenging or impossible to fully embrace the Bridal revelation or their own identity as the *Beloved* without first becoming grounded in the knowledge and experience of the love of Father God. Without that grounding, they just keep hoping they will someday find someone who will love them with unconditional love strong enough to heal their pain. The trauma they experienced as children often continues into their adulthood and manifests in the accumulation of more and more pain as relationships continue to fall apart or the cycle of abuse is repeated.

As my wife and I have traveled and taught this message, we have seen many people, both men and women, healed of the trauma of sexual abuse by inviting them to envision themselves crawling into the safe bed of Father God. It's a difficult step to take because images of their abuser almost always come instantly to mind. As we pray, our expectation is that they will go beyond the image of their abuser and experience a healing flood of love that comes from their heavenly Father. I don't want to trivialize the healing process by saying that the road to wholeness is always as easy as one step of faith. Sometimes it is - but sometimes the healing comes more slowly over time. I have come to believe that the story of Abishag was placed in the Bible to show us that *Becoming the Beloved* is not just an apprehension of certain knowledge, but it is also the transformation and healing of our hearts by a revelation of God's unconditional love - *both as our Father and as our Bridegroom.*

Abishag: From Scarecrow to Queen

Over time, Solomon was captivated by Abishag's beauty and allure. They eventually became betrothed, and the *Song* is, for the most part, the poetic chronicle of their marriage from the point of their betrothal to the consummation of their love. The rise of Abishag from an unknown farm girl to Queen of Israel is a true "rags to riches" story. It is a story that speaks to the very heart of the Gospel and our own undeserved advancement from sinner to saint. In the *Song*, the bride says that her brothers made her the "keeper of the vineyards"[118] which was the most menial kind of work. I believe her brothers represent the voice of dead religion which tells us that what God wants from us is only hard work. As the vineyard keeper, she was given a piece of tattered cloth and would squat on the dirt among the rows of grape vines all day

---

[118] Song of Songs 1:6

long in the blistering heat. When birds came to eat the fruit, she would jump to her feet and wave the cloth to scare them away. In essence, she was nothing more than a human scarecrow. She could never have dreamed that one day she would be delivered from the harsh reality of her life to stand beside the King of Israel under the wedding canopy. It is equally hard to imagine that you and I will one day be summoned to (what the Bible calls) the Marriage of the Lamb![119] It was by sovereign election that Abishag was chosen and then taken from the vineyard to live in the palace. It is by grace and election that we too are saved:

> *"He has delivered us from the power of darkness, and conveyed us into the kingdom of the Son of His love."*[120]

It is certain that Solomon would never have met Abishag had she not been summoned in the beginning to serve his father. In the same way, Jesus said, *"No one can come to me unless the Father who sent Me draws him."*[121] According to Jewish wedding customs, it was the bridegroom's father who acted as matchmaker. He was the one who initiated the betrothal on behalf of his son.

King David's Vision of the Bride

As King David's vision of the royal wedding unfolds in Psalm 45, he describes the bride's arrival for her wedding.

> The king's daughter is all glorious within: her clothing is of wrought gold. She shall be brought unto the king in raiment of needlework: the virgins her companions that follow her shall be brought unto thee. With gladness and

[119] Revelation 19:7
[120] Colossians 1:13
[121] John 6:44

> rejoicing shall they be brought: they shall enter into the king's palace.[122]

The glory of the Bride is not like the vain glory men bestow upon one another for their achievements. Her glory is found "within." Her wedding garment was made in such a way that threads of purest gold[123] were woven into the fabric. Gold is considered the metal of divinity, and the interwoven nature of the Bride's garment is an allusion to the joining of the nature of God with that of His Bride. The two become one flesh, and indeed, the Apostle Peter declared this truth when he wrote that we have become "partakers of the divine nature."[124]

Once, while visiting England, my wife and I took a tour of Windsor Castle. As we were viewing the famous Crown Jewels, we came to a large glass case which displayed the Queen's coronation dress. It was an exquisite creation of interwoven gold. As I gazed upon the beauty of the garment, I thought of what our royal wedding dress will look like at the end of the age! If the interwoven gold of an earthly queen can take one's breath away, how much more magnificent will our wedding garments be?

Shunammite or Shulamite?

Another similarity between Abishag and the Shulamite is their names. Abishag was called the Shunammite, while the bride in the *Song of Songs* is called the Shulamite. Although both words look and sound very much alike, they have very different meanings which we will explore.

---

[122] Psalm 45:13-15 RSV

[123] Psalm 45:9 states that the gold was mined from the famous gold-producing region of Ophir that is located in modern day Yemen. The gold of Ophir was of the finest quality.

[124] 2 Peter 1:4 KJV

Shunammite

Shunammite is simply a word that denotes the village of Abishag's birth. She came from Shunem, which was located in Galilee.[125] Shunem was located in the territory of land given to the tribe of Issachar. This in itself is highly significant because the tribe of Issachar was a prophetic tribe who understood God's dispensational dealings with Israel. It is said that they were *"men who had understanding of the times, to know what Israel ought to do."*[126] Those who will comprise the end-time Bridal Company will be distinguished by their ability to understand the prophetic significance of the time in which they live. While others will be caught unprepared at the coming of the Lord, the Bride will have "made herself ready."[127] She both understands the uniqueness of the time in which she lives and knows what to do with the time she is given. The bride in the *Song* is said to be she who "looks forth like the dawn."[128] This means that her eyes are looking eastward and scanning the horizon with expectancy toward the place where the sun [Son] will first appear. At the end of the age, while most of the Church will yawn with disinterest concerning the return of the Lord, the *Beloved* will fix her joyful hope and longing gaze upon the imminent return of her Bridegroom!

Shulamite

In the first few verses of the *Song,* the bride is heard crying out for an experience of intimacy with her king. She pleads, "O that you would kiss me with the kisses of your mouth![129] But it's

---

[125] I Kings 1:1-4
[126] 1 Chronicles 12:32
[127] Revelation 19:7
[128] Song of Songs 6:10 KJV
[129] Song of Songs 1:2 RSV

not just the thrill of romance she seeks. Her deeper desire is to be in *covenant relationship* with her king. This is expressed in the verse which follows, in which she compares the value of her king's name to the holy anointing oil of the Temple. It's his *name* she truly wants because his name represents his *covenant.* When couples marry, wives receive their husband's name! The name "Shulamite" appears only once in the *Song* near the end of the book. All through the book, Solomon refers to his bride as his dove, his love and his beloved but never by her natural name, Abishag. When he finally does bestow upon her the spiritual name *Shulamite,* it is deeply significant. God often changed the names of those who encountered Him. Abram, which means "father," was changed to Abraham meaning "father of nations." Jacob, which means "deceiver," God changed to Israel which means "prince with God." Solomon makes a similar change to Abishag's name by changing Shunnamite to Shulamite. By doing so, he honors her request to possess his own name! The name *Shulamite* is the perfect feminine compliment of Solomon's own name! Solomon means "peace." Shulamite means "one who has been made to know peace." In essence, Solomon gave his bride his own name as a representation of giving her his own nature.

9

THE BETROTHAL

And the two shall become one flesh.
Ephesians 5:31

Ancient Paths

It is always a good idea to seek to understand the cultural background of the events of the Bible. The ancient Jewish wedding customs provide a rich backdrop to the story-line of the *Song of Songs* and help us understand the progression of the story from the point of the couple's engagement until they consummate their love. It also enables us to look ahead to see how the marriage of Jesus and His Bride will take place at the end of the age.

My first exposure to these customs came when I was asked to officiate at a wedding where many of the Jewish traditions were incorporated into a non-Jewish ceremony. It was a new experience for our entire church to witness the couple saying their vows beneath a beautiful wedding canopy.

Kiddushin and Nissuin

The Jewish wedding progressed in two parts. The first part is called the *kiddushin,* and the second part is called the *nissuin.*

Kiddushin

The kiddushin began when a couple become engaged and

ended on their wedding night. When a couple fell in love, the young man went to his father and expressed his desire to marry. The father then became the overseer of the process of the kiddushin.

The Betrothal Meal

The purpose of the kiddushin was to satisfy the *legalities* of the marriage. To accomplish this, the father arranged a meeting with the father of the prospective bride to discuss the details of the wedding. Soon after this the young woman would come to the bridegroom's home to share a *betrothal meal.* An extravagant meal was provided and paid for by the groom's father in hopes of impressing the young woman and gaining her agreement to wed. Meals were common ways in which people engaged in contracts in ancient times. This is one reason the hyper-religious Jews became so enraged with Jesus when He ate with sinners.[130] In their culture, eating with someone was tantamount to entering into a covenant with them. When Jesus introduced His New Covenant, He also chose the setting of a meal to do so - the *Passover meal.*

The Marriage Contract

Once the meal ended, the bridegroom proposed marriage by offering the woman a written contract, called the *ketuba.* This was a legal document which spelled out in detail the obligations the bridegroom was willing to perform for his bride. It included such things as her inheritance rights, provisions of food and clothing and even conjugal rights. The bride, on the other hand, was not required to make any promises whatsoever to her

---

[130] Matthew 9:11

husband. The ketubah was read aloud to the bride, and then she was given a moment to consider her answer. It is commonly assumed that in ancient times a bride's husband was chosen *for* her and she was bound to marry whomever she was told. Actually, Jewish women were protected both by the Law and custom. A bride *always* had the right of refusal. If she did agree to the conditions of the wedding contract, it became hers to keep. At any time during her marriage, if her husband failed to live up to the promises he had made to her, she could take him to court and demand her rights!

The Bride's Price

An important part of the ketubah was the offering of the *mohar,* also called "the bride's price." This was an amount of money or another form of exchange the bridegroom was willing to pay for his bride. The amount was not considered equivalent to the worth of the bride. It could be a large or small sum, depending on the bridegroom's financial means. The reason for the exchange was two-fold. It was compensation to the bride's father for his loss. But, there was also a romantic meaning symbolized in the paying of the mohar. For Adam to have *his* bride, he was required to give up a literal part of his flesh and bone. He had to be willing to experience a lessening of himself in order to have his bride. By paying the bride's price, the bridegroom symbolically reenacted the costly sacrifice of Adam.

The Cup of Acceptance

If the bride accepted the ketubah and the mohar price, the next part of the kiddushin was called the offering of the *kiddush cup,* also called the "*cup of acceptance.*" The bridegroom poured wine into a silver cup, drank half of it, and then offered the remainder to his prospective bride. If she refused the drink, then the kiddushin ended without a betrothal being accomplished. If, on the other hand, she *did* take the cup and drink from it, the betrothal was instantly sealed. In fact, the moment the wine touched her lips, she became a legally married woman! All of her property as well as her debts became the legal property of her husband. Even though the actual wedding ceremony would not take place for about a year, the betrothal was legally binding. For it to be undone after that point, a legal divorce would have to be obtained. It was during the time between the betrothal and the ceremony that Mary became pregnant by the Holy Spirit. The Bible says that Joseph first considered "putting her away." This did not mean that he wanted to *send her away* to another town to escape the scandal. Being "put away" was a term which meant "to obtain a divorce."

The Parting and the Oath

Once the betrothal was sealed, the father retired from the room so that the couple could be alone to talk about their future plans. This part of the marriage custom was called *"the parting."*

During their year of separation, they would prepare themselves for married life. The man's responsibilities included building a place for them to live. Usually this would be a simple room built onto the existing home of his father, where they would live until they could afford to build their own home. In addition to this, the bridegroom had to work hard to earn enough money to support them for a full year after marriage, because Jewish law prohibited a newly married man from working at a job or going to war for a full year.

> When a man has taken a new wife, he shall not go out to war or be charged with any business; he shall be free at

home one year, and bring happiness to his wife whom he has taken.[131]

The bride used her time of separation to learn domestic skills which included the management of the family business. After sharing their hearts and plans, the bridegroom would not leave until he gave his wineskin to his bride and bound himself with a traditional oath.[132] He promised not to drink wine again until he had finished building their home. Some of the last words of Jesus to His disciples agree with this wedding custom as He told them, "I will not drink of the fruit of the vine, until the kingdom of God shall come."[133]

The Mikvah

Not long after the betrothal had been sealed, the bride's friends planned a party in her honor. The centerpiece of the party was a ceremonial bath called a "*mikvah,*" which was a baptism performed for the purpose of consecration. The bride would disrobe and lie down in the water. Her friends would gather around and push her downward until she was completely immersed. Once submerged, she opened her eyes and spread her fingers and toes so that the water could touch every part of her body. After that, her attendants dressed her in a special linen robe provided beforehand by her bridegroom. It was his first gift to her. As the *Beloved of Christ,* we also have been provided a robe of righteousness by our Bridegroom!

Let us be glad and rejoice, and give Him glory: for the

---

[131] Deuteronomy 24:5

[132] During the time of Solomon and even Christ, men carried wineskins tied to their belts.

[133] Luke 22:18 NKJV

marriage of the Lamb has come, and his wife has made herself ready. *And to her it was granted to be arrayed in fine linen, clean and bright: for the fine linen is the righteous acts of the saints*.[134] [emphasis added]

The Veiling of the Bride

Before the party ended, the bride's friends presented her with a veil designed to cover her face except for her eyes. From that day forward, she was required to wear it whenever she was outside. The veil was a sign that she had become a married woman. It said to the other men of the village, "You may no longer desire me because I am now consecrated." Today, the true spiritual Bride is readily identified by her singular devotion to her Bridegroom. Jesus has called us to be veiled in the sense that we are to be "in the world but not of the world."[135]

The Adorning of the Bride

Even though the couple would not begin to live together for a year or so, they were legally married once the kiddushin was achieved. The bridegroom became responsible for the material needs of his bride from the moment of their betrothal. The provision he made for her during their time of separation was called the "*mattan*" also known as the "adorning of the bride." The linen garment given to her at the time of her mikvah was the first gift bestowed upon the bride, but it was certainly not the last! Throughout the separation period, gifts of jewels, rings, gold, and silver were customarily given in support of his beloved!

---

[134] Revelation 19:7-8
[135] John 17:16 Author's paraphrase of NKJV

The Groomsmen

Unlike our modern weddings, ancient Jewish weddings had *two* groomsmen who were called the *"friends of the bridegroom."* One groomsman attended the bridegroom while the other attended the bride. The bride's attendant was called the *"philos"* (φίλος.) During the days of the bride's preparation the philos, as a go-between, had more actual contact with the bride than the bridegroom himself. Thus, he had to be a well trusted friend! If the bride had a need, she told it to the philos, and he relayed that information to the bridegroom. The bridegroom, in turn, gave the philos whatever the bride needed, and he delivered it to her. It is clear that this is a figure of the role of the Holy Spirit! He now acts on Christ's behalf to prepare us for our wedding. Jesus said of the Holy Spirit that He "will take of what is Mine and declare (deliver) it to you."[136] Whenever we have a need, all we have to do is let our Bridegroom know by praying in the Holy Spirit!

The Nissuin

As already stated, the kiddushin stage of the betrothal was basically concerned with the legalities of the marriage. After the year-long separation, it was time for the wedding ceremony and the consummation of the contract. This latter part of the marriage was called the *"nissuin."*

Abduction of the Bride

As unusual as it seems to us today, the bride was not

[136] John 16:14

allowed to know the exact date of her wedding. She would have a sense that the day was approaching, but the exact timing of the event was known only by the father of the bridegroom. Once he was satisfied that the home was ready and that enough finances had been set aside, he would direct his son to secretly gather the wedding party to their home. This usually occurred late at night in order to surprise the bride. After the guests were assembled, they became participants in a wedding "drama" called *"the abduction of the bride."* In this drama, the bridegroom played the part of a conquering king! It began when his father placed a garland upon his head and told him to go and call his bride to their wedding. At this point, some of the men of the wedding party would lift the bridegroom onto a wooden platform called an "aperion" where he would be carried in procession to the bride's house. Alongside the aperion, the men would march in military pomp with swords strapped to their thighs. They acted as the bridegroom's personal army. Today, in modern Jewish weddings, this custom is still observed when both the bridegroom and bride are lifted into the air and danced around the room while seated on wooden chairs. The procession moved through the village streets with torches and tambourines. Wedding songs filled the air as the noisy crowd made its way to the house of the bride. To make sure she was aware of their arrival, a friend of the bridegroom[137] ran slightly ahead of the party until he was near the bride's house. Then he blew a ram's horn[138] and shouted, "Behold, the bridegroom is coming!" The bride would awaken, gather her belongings, which included her oil lamp, and run out to meet her bridegroom in the street. Once there, she was lifted onto the aperion and carried back to the father's house where the wedding commenced. The bridegroom's coming for his bride riding in the air is a picture of Christ appearing in the clouds to abduct His

---

[137] This was the second groomsman called the "friend of the bridegroom"
[138] The ram's horn was called a "shofar."

Bride at the time of the Rapture.

The Wedding Canopy

Arriving at the bridegroom's house, the bride would see that everything had been prepared for the ceremony in advance of her arrival. To exchange their vows, the bride and bridegroom stepped beneath a square canopy made of fabric called a *"chuppah"* (pronounced hoopa.) Today, the chuppah remains the centerpiece of most Jewish weddings. It represents the overshadowing Presence of God's glory that was present at Sinai when He married Israel. As they stepped beneath the chuppah, guests spread palm and myrtle branches before them. It was a scene reminiscent of Jesus' entrance into Jerusalem before His passion.[139] Coins were also tossed at the couple to be gathered up later as gifts.

The Encompassing of the Man

Beneath the chuppah, the bride would leave her bridegroom's side and walk slowly around him seven times. This tradition is called *"the encompassing of the man."* The origin of this custom is uncertain but seems to be linked to a verse in Jeremiah which speaks of a woman circling around a man.[140] Some liken this to the story of how the walls of Jericho fell down once the Israelites had encompassed it. The wall of propriety which had separated the bride from her bridegroom for a year was now coming down. Before this night she was like a walled city. Now she is a city to be "taken."

There is a deeper meaning to this obscure custom. The

---

[139] John 12:13

[140] See Jeremiah 31:22

Hebrew word for "helpmate" is the word *"ezer"* (רזע). Ezer comes from the root word *'azar* (רזע) which means *"to gird, to surround, to walk in a circle, to establish boundaries for defense."* It appears that God gave Adam his helpmate to remind him to remain within his proper boundaries. She was, in essence, the "boundary keeper" in the Garden. Perhaps this explains why the serpent approached *her* instead of the man. She was the one who operated in that realm of authority. It seems that wives still possess this "instinct of Eve" to encircle their husbands with their love, care and concern for their well-being. It is estimated that fifty to eighty percent of all doctor appointments for *men* are actually arranged for them by their *wives*! Obviously if it weren't for wives, there would be fewer husbands! When a Jewish bride encompasses her bridegroom, she is saying, "I will not fail, as Eve did, in guarding our marriage."

The Breaking of the Glass

Another tradition with an obscure origin and meaning occurs at the end of the wedding ceremony, when a wine glass, wrapped in a napkin, is placed beneath the bridegroom's foot so he can crush it with his heel. Tradition says that this is done to remember the destruction of the Temple. I would suggest that it might also represent the final crushing of Satan's head beneath the heel of Christ.

> [God speaking] I will put enmity between you (the serpent) and the woman, and between your seed and her seed (Messiah); he shall bruise your head, and you shall bruise his heel. [141] [emphasis added]

[141] Genesis 3:15 RSV

The Wedding Chamber

After the ceremony beneath the chuppah, the bridegroom would accompany his bride to a special room in his father's house called the *"chedar"* (חדר) or *"the bride's chamber."* The bridegroom would have taken great care in furnishing and decorating the chedar to make it a pleasant and romantic place for them to share their love. Food, water, wine and everything else they might need was waiting for them inside the room. Today, modern Jewish couples honor this tradition by observing what is called *"yichud."* Following the ceremony, the couple slips away and spends a few minutes in *yichud* (or seclusion.) In ancient times, however, the seclusion lasted a full seven days in which the couple remained totally hidden from sight. Immediately upon entering the chedar, one of the best men appointed for this duty, would position himself just outside the door awaiting word from the groom that the marriage had been sexually consummated. Once accomplished, the news of the consummation was told to the wedding guests. A party would begin, and it would last for seven days.

The Seclusion of the Couple

The prophetic significance of the seven day seclusion period cannot be overlooked. You will recall that the bride is lifted into the air and carried to her wedding while seated with her bridegroom upon an aperion. This is a beautiful, prophetic portrayal of Jesus coming for His Bride at the time of the Rapture. The Bible says that we shall be caught up in the clouds to meet the Lord *in the air.*[142] Upon the bride's arrival in heaven, the wedding will commence. The Couple will enter their wedding *chedar,*

---

[142] 1 Thessalonians 4:16-17

where they will be hidden away - not for seven days - but for seven years while the world enters the period known as the Great Tribulation. In the 26th chapter of Isaiah we read:

> Come, my people, enter your chambers, and shut your doors behind you; hide yourselves for a little while until the wrath is past.[143] [emphasis added]

The Hebrew word for "chambers" is the word "chedar" or "bride's chamber." Isaiah saw the end-time Bride of Christ entering her bridal chamber to be hidden safely away while God's wrath passed over the earth.

The Eighth Day

The passage in Isaiah 26 continues:

> For behold, the LORD is coming forth out of His place to punish the inhabitants of the earth for their iniquity, and the earth will disclose the bloodshed upon her, and will no more cover her slain.[144] [emphasis added]

According to Strong's concordance, the Hebrew word for "place" used in this verse is the word *"maqowm"* and it comes from a root word which is used to describe the *pudenda* (sexual organs) of a woman. This verse implies that, during the period of the Great Tribulation, Christ will be focused on consummating His marriage with His Bride. Only when the seven years is finished, will He leave His wedding chamber to render judgment to the nations.

---

[143] Isaiah 26:20-21 RSV
[144] Isaiah 26:20-21 RSV

A New Beginning

The number eight in the Bible represents a day of new beginning. God created the world in six days, rested on the seventh, and the *eighth* day was the beginning of the new week. When God destroyed the world with the flood, there were *eight* people in Noah's family who were saved to replenish the earth as a new beginning. Likewise, the bridegroom and bride are not seen again until the *eighth* day when they emerge to rejoin the wedding party. At the end of the Tribulation period, Jesus, accompanied by His Bride, will come "out of His place" (Isaiah 26:21) to punish His enemies. At that time, the visage of the Bride will be like that of her Bridegroom as they ride into the final battle of the earth. In the *Song of Songs,* Solomon describes his bride as being as "terrible as an army with banners"[145] and indeed, we will return with Christ as part of His magnificent, victorious army!

The Honeymoon Tent

After the wedding was complete, the couple enjoyed a protracted honeymoon period. As already stated, the bridegroom was forbidden to work at any job for a full year so that he could give his bride his undivided love and attention.[146] During this time, they traveled around the countryside living in a tent called an *"ohel"* (לֹהא). The honeymoon excursions of Solomon and his bride are described in the *Song of Songs,* chapter seven:

> I am my beloved's, and his desire is toward me. Come, my beloved, let us go forth to the field; Let us lodge in the villages. Let us get up early to the vineyards; Let us see if the vine has budded; Whether the grape blossoms are

[145] Song of Songs 6:4,10 KJV
[146] Deuteronomy 24:5

> open, And the pomegranates are in bloom. there will I give thee my love.[147]

A brief study of the word "ohel" will lend deeper insight into the relationship the Bride has with her Bridegroom. When Isaac met Rebekah as she returned from Haran, he immediately brought her into his mother's tent (lit. ohel) and she became his wife.[148] When David pitched his Tent of Worship at Zion, the word for that tent is also the word "ohel."

> David built houses for himself in the City of David; and he prepared a place for the ark of God, and pitched a tent (אהל - ohel) for it.[149]

The Tent of David was characterized by its unprecedented access to the Presence of God. The Ark of the Covenant was placed in the center of the Tent with no curtain to hide it from view. Around the Ark, the priests, appointed by David, worshipped the Lord continuously.

The Ohel Mo'ed

Although the tent that David pitched for the Ark was an ohel, the Tabernacle which Moses built was called the "*mishkan.*" Moses actually built two tabernacles. One was the Tabernacle (mishkan) located inside the camp of Israel and the other was a simple tent called the "Ohel Mo'ed" which he pitched *outside* the camp. It was called "The Tent of Meeting" because it was there that Moses actually met and communed with the Lord.

Jewish tradition says that when God first appeared to

---

147 Song of Songs 7:10-12
148 Genesis 24:67
149 1 Chronicles 15:1

Moses, it was outdoors in a burning bush encompassed by fire. It was a representation of God's power and glory but not His actual Person. Later, God met with Moses *inside* the Ohel Mo'ed because there He spoke with him "face to face as a man speaks with his friend."[150] The more intimate we grow in our communion with God, the more concealed our lives become. There is an outward experience of the Presence of God and also one that is inward. This is why Jesus called the place of prayer a *secret place* or a "closet."[151] Intimacy, by its nature, requires levels of concealment. Many are content to attend a conference or be in a meeting where the power and anointing of God is felt. That is equivalent to meeting God at the burning bush. While not seeking to diminish the importance of such encounters, it must be said that the Bride's favorite place is not with the many in the *mishkan* but in the secret place of prayer and worship. Her place is in the *Ohel Mo'ed - the honeymoon tent!*

[150] Exodus 33:11
[151] Matthew 6:6

10

THE BETROTHAL OF JESUS

For me the Heavenly Bridegroom waits,
To make me pure of sin.
The Sabbaths of Eternity,
One Sabbath deep and wide
A light upon the shining sea,
The Bridegroom with His bride!
From St. Agnes' Eve
By Alfred Lord Tennyson

The Betrothal of Jesus

As I studied the ancient Jewish wedding customs, I began to wonder if the same process of kiddushin could be observed in the life of Jesus. Not only did I find the pattern in the Gospel accounts, but I was amazed to discover that Jesus meticulously fulfilled each step of betrothal in proper sequence!

The Betrothal Meal

You will recall that once the son found a young woman he wished to marry, his father was the one who initiated the betrothal on behalf of his son by preparing the betrothal meal. With this in mind, I looked to the Gospels to see if I could find a meal Jesus shared with his disciples that might serve as a betrothal meal. But according to custom, it had to be a meal that neither Jesus nor his disciples prepared. When I read over the details of the Passover meal, I knew I had found it!

> Then came the day of Unleavened Bread, on which the Passover lamb had to be sacrificed. So Jesus sent Peter and John, saying, "Go and prepare the Passover for us, that we may eat it." They said to him, "Where will you have us prepare it?" He said to them, "Behold, when you have entered the city, a man carrying a jar of water will meet you; follow him into the house which he enters, and tell the householder, 'The Teacher says to you, Where is the guest room, where I am to eat the passover with my disciples?' And he will show you a large upper room furnished; there make ready."[152] And they went, and found it as he had told them; and they prepared the Passover.[153]

There is a hint of intrigue in this story that I find compelling. The disciples were told to follow a mysterious man who was carrying a pitcher of water. They were told to enter the same house the man entered and there they would find a furnished room and a Passover meal that had *already* been prepared for them. Jesus provided neither the furnishings nor the meal. That was not His obligation as the Bridegroom. Neither did His disciples make any of the preparations. That was not the duty of the Bride either. Everything was done *for* them by the mysterious unseen hands of Father God. You might notice that Jesus does tell them to "make ready" but this is a reference to making *themselves* ready to eat the meal. Jews did not eat until they had performed ceremonial washings.

---

[152] This probably refers to making themselves *personally* ready to eat the Passover by ceremonial washing.
[153] Luke 22:7-13 RSV

Notice too, that the room is called a "large upper room." The large, upper room on earth was a representation of the Father's house from above to which the Bride (represented by the disciples) had been invited.

The Ketubah and the Bride's Price

During the Passover meal, Jesus offered His followers a legal contract (*ketubah*) called the New Covenant. As part of His covenant, He also stated the mohar. It was the price He was willing to pay to have them as His Bride. The Bible tells us that we no longer belong to ourselves because we have been "bought with a price" (mohar.)[154]

> ...this is My blood of the new covenant, which is shed for many for the remission of sins.[155]

Likewise, the Apostle Peter declared,

> You know that you were ransomed from the futile ways inherited from your fathers, not with perishable things such as silver or gold, but with the *precious blood of Christ*, like that of a lamb without blemish or spot.[156]

The Cup of Acceptance

Jesus continued to follow the pattern of the kiddushin by next offering His disciples the cup of acceptance called the *"kiddush cup ."*

---

[154] 1 Corinthians 6:20b
[155] Matthew 26:28
[156] 1 Peter 1:18-19 RSV

> *And He took a cup*, and when He had given thanks He gave it to them, saying, "Drink of it, all of you; for this is My blood of the covenant, which is poured out for many for the forgiveness of sins.[157] [emphasis added]

This was perhaps the most crucial moment in the history of mankind. The redemption of the world literally hung in the balance the moment Jesus pushed the cup of His Covenant in front of them. Would they accept or refuse the cup of their Bridegroom? Remember, brides always had the "right of refusal." When they took the cup and drank, the marriage between Messiah and His Bride was sealed! An agreement was forged between heaven and earth! The marriage of Christ to His Bride became a legal reality in the realm of the Spirit.

The Mikvah

By now I hope you see that each step of the betrothal custom was meticulously followed and fulfilled by Jesus during the Passover meal. The bride's *mikvah* was no exception.

> And during [the Passover] supper, when the devil had already put it into the heart of Judas Iscariot, Simon's son, to betray Him, Jesus, knowing that the Father had given all things into His hands, and that He had come from God and was going to God, rose from supper, laid aside His garments, and girded Himself with a towel. Then He poured water into a basin, and began to wash the disciples' feet... [158]

When the disciples followed the mysterious man into the room

---

[157] Matthew 26:27-28 RSV
[158] John 13:2-5 RSV

where the Passover meal awaited them, that man was carrying a pitcher of water. The pitcher of water was there for the special purpose of providing pure water for the Bride's mikvah. After the disciples had accepted the Lord's kiddush cup, He invited them to the fulfillment of the next step in the process of betrothal. Putting aside his garments, Jesus began to wash His disciple's feet. Not understanding the true meaning of what was happening, Peter protested.

> He came to Simon Peter; and Peter said to Him, "Lord, do you wash my feet?" Jesus answered him, "What I am doing you do not know now, but afterward you will understand." Peter said to Him, "You shall never wash my feet." Jesus answered him, "If I do not wash you, you have no part in me." 9 Simon Peter said to Him, "Lord, not my feet only but also my hands and my head!" (John 13:6-9 RSV) [emphasis added]

When Peter finally did grasp the revelation that the washing he was receiving at the hands of Jesus was actually a ritual *mikvah* he exclaimed,

> *"Lord, not my feet only but also my hands and my head!"*

What had begun as a "foot washing" suddenly became an "all over washing." *Fingers and toes spread. Eyes wide open!*

The Parting and the Oath

How amazed I was to see each step of the betrothal fulfilled without fail.

Once the Passover meal had ended, Jesus began to share

His *"parting words"* with His Bride. He even bound Himself to the traditional oath:

> And He took a cup, and when He had given thanks He gave it to them, saying, "Drink of it, all of you; for this is My blood of the covenant, which is poured out for many for the forgiveness of sins. *I tell you I shall not drink again of this fruit of the vine until that day when I drink it new with you in my Father's kingdom.* [159] [emphasis added]

The House that Jesus Built

The remainder of Jesus' parting words can be found in John 16 and 17. There, He comforts them concerning His leaving and promises to return for them once He has finished preparing a place for them to live:

> Let not your heart be troubled: ye believe in God, believe also in me. In my Father's house are many mansions: if it were not so, I would have told you. *I go to prepare a place for you.* And if I go and prepare a place for you, I will come again, and receive you unto myself; that where I am, there ye may be also. (John 14:1-2) [emphasis added]

In Jesus' time, families often lived in a bee-hive of buildings called *insulas.* A courtyard provided a common area and around the courtyard many rooms were built to accommodate extended family members. When sons married, they simply built an addition onto the insula, which became their home. This is clearly the meaning of Jesus' statement about the many "mansions" in his Father's house.

---

[159] Matthew 26:27-29 RSV

The Heavenly "Philos"

Jesus also used His parting words to introduce His disciples to the Holy Spirit who would act as the go-between, called the "philos." You will recall that the job of the philos was to adorn the bride with gifts (matten) from her bridegroom. Likewise, the Holy Spirit has been sent to adorn the Bride of Christ with spiritual gifts and provide for her daily needs:

> Nevertheless I tell you the truth: it is to your advantage that I go away, for if I do not go away, the Counselor will not come to you; but if I go, I will send Him to you…When the Spirit of truth comes, He will guide you into all the truth; for He will not speak on His own authority, but whatever He hears He will speak, and He will declare to you the things that are to come. He will glorify me, for He will take what is Mine and declare it to you. [160]

> Now we have received not the spirit of the world, but the Spirit which is from God, that we might understand *the gifts bestowed on us by God.*[161] [emphasis added]

The Nissuin

When Jesus concluded His parting words, the kiddushin was brought to an end. The second part of the betrothal, called the "nissuin" now awaits fulfillment. It will begin when Jesus returns from heaven to secretly abduct His Bride to her wedding. If the Father and the Son faithfully executed the demands of the kiddushin, should we not expect Jesus to return at the appropriate

[160] John 16:7,13-14 RSV
[161] 1 Corinthians 2:12 RSV

time to fulfill the terms of the nissuin as well?

Loving His Appearance

Once, after I had delivered a teaching on the subject of the return of Jesus, I was approached by a young woman who asked me if I really thought that Jesus might return in her lifetime. When I told her that I thought it was probable, a look of disappointment washed over her face. She told me, "I'm young and there are things I want to do. I want to get married and have a family." I think her response reflects how many Christians feel about the imminent return of Christ. But imagine that soon after a young couple marry, the husband is sent to war. For months they are forced to live apart, communicating only by long distance. Then one day she receives a phone call. Her husband tells her that he is on his way home at last! In fact, he will be arriving home within hours. Suppose upon hearing this, his wife replied, "Do you really have to come home today? I have made plans to go shopping with my friends. Could you wait and come back another day?" Would you think that bride truly loved her husband? *Of course not.* Yet that is often the very attitude many Christians have in regard to the return of Jesus. We will never love the *appearing* of the Lord until first we fall in love with the Lord, Himself. I believe one of the hallmarks of those who possess a Bridal heart is that they do not fear the second coming of Jesus - *they yearn for it!* The true Bride watches the signs of the times and waits with rapt attention for the moment when the shofar will sound and she will be caught up together with her Bridegroom in the air. *Hallelujah. Even so, Come, Lord Jesus!*

The Deeper Revelation

But let's take a deeper look at what really took place when

Jesus initiated and achieved the *kiddushin* with His disciples.
One of the worst distortions of Scripture is the story of the fall of man in the Garden in Eden. Most of us were taught that the woman was deceived by the serpent into disobeying God first. Then she lured and deceived her husband into eating as well. There is an important problem with this interpretation. The Bible clearly states that Adam was ***not*** deceived when he joined his wife in eating what had been forbidden by God.

> For Adam was formed first, then Eve. And Adam was not deceived, but the woman being deceived, fell into transgression.[162] [emphasis added]

This is not a minor point of theology. Since God is "imaging" something through Adam, it is important that we see the correct image. If Adam was not deceived when he ate the forbidden fruit, that means he did so as a *choice* of his free will. He *chose* to eat, knowing full well the consequences of his actions! The question then becomes, "Why?" *Why would he choose to eat the fruit knowing the horrible result that would follow?* To answer this question, we must entertain an alternative to the story we have been told.

Consider how purely innocent the man and woman must have been in their original state. Sin and its disastrous effect were totally foreign to them. But at the moment the woman's lips touched the fruit of the tree, something happened inside of her. Her innocence became corrupted in that instant. Immortality put on mortality, and for the first time in her life, she felt shame and fear. The harsh realization of God's words echoed in her mind, reminding her that now she would "surely die."[163]

---

[162] 1 Timothy 2:13-14

[163] Genesis 2:17

If we accept the story as it has been traditionally interpreted, the woman becomes a cohort of the deceiver. She approaches her husband as an emissary of Satan with the intent of enticing him to sin. I will show you why this could not possibly be the correct interpretation. But to do so, we must contemplate a different scenario.

Consider the possibility that when the woman realized what she had done, she ran to Adam with the fruit still in her hand. She ran to him, not with the intent of deceiving him, but to seek his help instead. We can only imagine the fear resonating in her voice as she confessed the terrible thing she had done:

> *"Adam! Help me! The serpent deceived me and I ate! I have done what God warned us not to do, and now, I'm going to die!"*[164]

By no choice of his own, Adam was thrust into a dilemma. He had not yet eaten and so he could continue to live forever with God in the Garden. To do so however, meant he would have to live forever *without* his bride. She was going to die, just as God had warned and now she cried out for her husband to help her. As an ultimate act of love, Adam reached out, took the fruit from her hand, and ate it. He chose to die *with* his bride rather than live without her. The choice Adam made was not made by deception. *It was the choice of selfless love.* The Bible says nothing about Adam being deceived. Instead, it says he ate as a result of *hearkening* to the voice of his wife.[165] The Hebrew word translated as "hearkened" is the word *shama* (שמע) and it has nothing to do with being deceived. In fact it has the opposite meaning. It means to "give careful attention to, to listen in order to make a judicial decision, to understand at the deepest level." *Shama* is the same word which begins the most important prayer in Judaism:

---

[164] Author's conjecture
[165] Genesis 3:17

> Hear (shama) O Israel, the Lord is our God, the Lord is One.[166]

Jesus, the Last Adam

Jesus, like Adam, had a choice to make. His Bride (mankind) had sinned and was doomed to die. He could live forever with His Father. But to do so meant He would have to live forever *without* His Bride. So, in order to save her, He would have to identify *with* her in her sin. He willingly "tasted death on behalf of every man."[167] In the same way Adam "hearkened" to the cry of his bride, Jesus hearkens to the voice of everyone who cries to Him for help:

> And it shall be that whoever ***calls*** on the name of the Lord shall be saved.[168] [emphasis added]

A Legal Transaction

In the same way the bride became legally married as soon as she drank from the kiddush cup, something legal transpired the moment Eve brought the forbidden fruit to her lips. God had given her a law and when she broke the law, it put into motion yet another law which the Bible calls the "law of sin and death."[169] Eve's communion with God was broken by touching the fruit of disobedience to her lips. In essence, she drank the covenant cup offered to her by the serpent. Mankind's communion with God was restored by the same method - only in reverse!

---

[166] Deuteronomy 6:4-9
[167] Hebrews 2:9
[168] Acts 2:21 RSV
[169] Romans 8:2

The Two Shall Become One

Because the bridegroom drank from the *kiddush* cup first, he left a little part of himself in the wine - a trace of his DNA mingled with the juice! When his bride took her first sip she welcomed the very first part of her husband inside of herself. At that moment, "the two [literally] became one flesh." For this very reason, the drinking of the kiddush cup was also known as drinking the "kiss from the cup."

In the *Song of Songs,* the Shulamite tells of the moment when her lips touched her own betrothal cup:

> Let him kiss me with the kisses of his mouth: For Your love is better than wine. [170]

She praises the superiority of his kiss above the savor and content of the wine itself. In other words, the little part of himself that he left in the wine when he drank from it caused an improvement to the quality *of* the wine! The first "kiss" an ancient Jewish couple shared was not mouth to mouth. It was the cup to the mouth of the bridegroom and then the mouth of the bride to the cup. Their first kiss was mingled and shared in a cup of covenant!

God Called "Them" Adam

A careful reading of the Bible reveals another fascinating fact concerning Adam and Eve:

> This is the book of the generations of Adam. In the day that God created man, in the likeness of God made He

[170] Song of Songs 1:2

> him; male and female created He them; and blessed them, and called ***their*** name Adam, in the day when they were created.[171] [emphasis added]

In order for Adam to accurately portray God's nature, he had to be created with both masculine and feminine attributes. In pointing to this, I am not attempting in any way to "feminize" God. Predominantly, the Scriptures present God in the masculine role as our Father. However, it should not be overlooked that there are also many references in the Bible in which God is portrayed with feminine characteristics. The name *El Shaddai* (ידש לא),[172] for instance, means "the breasted one, or the breast feeder." In the book of Deuteronomy, God compares Himself with a mother eagle nurturing her young.[173] Since the woman existed inside of man from the very beginning, this means that all of the feminine and masculine attributes were originally contained in the person of the man. Adam was the man that all women long for! Sensitive, caring, intuitive, and nurturing! But, alas, those qualities were removed and formed into woman, leaving man with a deficit for which only a woman can compensate. As an image of God, Adam shows forth that which existed in the heart of Christ before we ever came into existence. We were "in Christ" before the foundation of the world!

> Long before He laid down earth's foundations, He had us in mind, had settled on us as the focus of His love, to be made whole and holy by His love.[174]

Imagine that before God said, "Let there be light," He had already said, "Let there be YOU!" You are not the after-thought of

---

[171] Genesis 5:1-2 ASB
[172] Exodus 6:3
[173] Deuteronomy 32:11
[174] Ephesians 1:3-6 The Message

Creation - *you were the fore-thought!*

One Person Living in Two Bodies

The man and woman were so intrinsically and intimately connected, they were literally *one person living in two bodies*. This is seen in the fact that they were both called by the same name, "Adam."

> Male and female created He them; and blessed them, and called their name Adam, in the day when they were created.[175] [emphasis added]

In the Bible, names relate to the *nature* of a person or thing. Eve was not called "Eve" until after she sinned. Until that time, she shared the name of the man because they were synonymous in their nature. There existed the male Adam and the female Adam. After she sinned, however, a rift was created in her relationship with God and with her husband as well. Eve means "the mother of all." Her name changed because her destiny changed. No longer was she exclusively the helpmate of Adam. Now, she was to become the mother of mortal children as well.

The Sin Covenant

In a very real sense, the original sin of the man and woman was achieved by the two of them agreeing to enter into a covenant to sin and die together. As I have shown, the woman was initially deceived by the serpent, but the man sinned as an act of love. Likewise, even though Christ never sinned, He was willing (as an act of His will) to be *"made sin for us, so that we might be made the*

[175] Genesis 5:1-2 ASV

righteousness of God in Him."[176]

Adam and his wife enjoyed such perfect "oneness" they could not even fully sin apart from one another. Consider if Adam had not been moved by his wife's plea for help. Imagine if he had not joined her in disobeying God's command. What if he had simply walked away from her that day? Eventually she would have died alone and childless. There would have been no human race tainted with the original sin. It required the disobedience of both the woman *and* the man for sin to go beyond them and enter into the world. In the beginning, man and woman were made in the image of God. But after they sinned and once they began to procreate, the Bible says that they produced children made "in [their] own likeness, and after [their own] image."[177]

If Two on Earth Agree

Nothing is ever accomplished in the spiritual realm without a covenant. God never walked with man unless He first forged a covenant with that man. It takes at least two people coming into agreement for anything to be accomplished. That is why it was crucial for Jesus to seal a covenant with His disciples before leaving that final Passover meal. He sought their agreement with what He was about to do. It was vital that they drink His cup and accept His covenant as an act of their free will. Sin was brought into the world when a bride went to a tree and ate its fruit as an act of disobedience. In a magnificent reversal, sin was taken *out* of the world when a Bridegroom went to a tree (the Cross) and ate the fruit of obedience! Jesus told His Father, "Not my will, but Your's be done."[178]

---

[176] 2 Corinthians 5:21
[177] Genesis 5:3
[178] Luke 22:42 NIV

When Jesus came to earth, He had all the authority of heaven to go to the Cross and accomplish redemption for mankind. Yet He lacked one important – even vital thing. *He needed His Bride's covenant agreement!* In order to release the human race from the curse of sin which was brought into the world by a covenant forged between the first man and his bride, Jesus also needed His Bride's agreement to take sin *out of the world.*

Satan came to the Last Supper and watched with interest what happened. He knew if the disciples accepted the Covenant of Jesus, his doom was sealed. The Bible states that it was at the moment when they drank the cup that Satan entered into Judas.[179] The die then was cast in a plot to kill Jesus.

Look, however, at the wording found in John, chapter 13:

> Now before the feast of the Passover, when Jesus knew that His hour had come that He should depart from this world to the Father, having loved His own who were in the world, He loved them unto the end. And supper being ended, the devil having already put into the heart of Judas Iscariot, Simon's son, to betray Him; *Jesus knowing that the Father had given all things into His hands*, and that He had come from God, and was going to God. . .[180] [emphasis added]

"All things" were not yet delivered into the hands of Jesus by His Father ***UNTIL*** the moment the disciples accepted the wedding proposal and drank from the Lord's kiddush cup. Once they drank, then Jesus knew that He possessed not only the mandate of heaven to go to the Cross - *but also the agreement of*

---

[179] Luke 13:27
[180] John 13:1-3 NKJV

earth! All things were now delivered into His hands. In the same way it took both a bridegroom and bride to bring sin and death upon the human race, it took both the eternal Bridegroom *and* His Bride to take the curse of sin and death *out* of the human race. The implication of this is staggering! It means that we are not only the *recipients* of God's redemption; but also we are His *co-redemptive partners in the work of redemption!*

The Fragrance of the Bride

Just days before Jesus would endure the Cross, He traveled to the home of a man called Simon the Leper. This took place in the village of Bethany. While there, a woman identified historically as Mary of Bethany, entered the room and broke open an alabaster box filled with the equivalent of one year's wages worth of pure, liquid spikenard. She poured the copious oil upon the head of Christ until He was saturated with its essence and fragrance. Although chided by those present at the supper for making a "waste" of the oil, Christ revealed that she had come "beforehand" to prepare His body for the passion of the Cross. In other words, Mary's extravagant display of love and worship was fueled by a very real *revelation* of what Christ was about to suffer on her behalf. She was there to prepare His body for death and burial by saturating it with the fragrance of spikenard. The word "spikenard" is found in only two places in the whole of the Bible - in the *Song of Songs* and in this account of Mary's anointing of Jesus! In the *Song,* a beautiful prophetic preview of this Gospel account is foretold:

> While the king is at his table, my *spikenard* sends
> forth it's fragrance.[181][emphasis added]

---

[181] Song of Songs 1:12

The bride in the *Song* likens spikenard to her own fragrance. She calls it "my" spikenard. It was *her* perfume. In the Gospel accounts, we are told that the King (Jesus) was indeed seated at a table at the time of His anointing. By this act of love and worship, Mary is clearly identifiable as an archetype of the Bride of Christ. In a few days, Jesus would be arrested and mistreated. His body would be beaten until it was a bloody mass. He would be spat upon and dragged through the streets strewn with the excrement of animals. By the time He reached the Cross, the smell of death would be upon Him. The smell of sweat, dirt, filth, spittle and blood blended into a vile concoction. Once lifted upon the Cross, however, Jesus became aware of *another* fragrance; one so potent it overpowered the stench of His own death! Spikenard, the sweet smell of His Bride, was there as a constant reminder of *why* He had chosen to identify with her sin and death. Every time He inhaled, Jesus was reminded of the great reward that awaited Him on the other side of His suffering. Yes, we were there on the Cross with Him, symbolized by the spikenard on His body!

11

THE KISS

This done, he took the bride about the neck and kissed her lips with such a clamorous smack that at the parting, all the church did echo.
William Shakespeare

To Hunger or to Taste?

Oh, that the Church would be shaken awake by the echoing sound of a passionate kiss! We need to feel it reverberating within our hallowed halls and rigid walls of cold religious duty. We need to feel it flowing into us like an infusion of holy, reckless desire that will unshackle us from the loveless, passionless religious lives we've made for ourselves.

As I was driving home one evening, I listened to a well known Bible teacher on the radio. He was talking about how Christians should be wary of trusting their emotions and should cling to faith in God's Word instead. He spoke as if those two things were as incompatible as oil and water. In fact he taught that our emotions were the "enemy of our faith." How often I have heard this same teaching in one form or another in the course of my journey with God. *And how wrong it is!* God gave us our emotions for a reason. He has designed us to experience more than living on the dry side of perpetual hunger. He gives us our hunger so that He might fill it:

> Blessed are those who hunger and thirst for righteousness, *for they will be filled.*[182] [emphasis added]

Many of our contemporary worship songs speak of hungering after God. That is good, but perhaps we should think about crafting some songs that speak of the *satisfaction* of being filled with Him as well. Communing with our Bridegroom is more than the experience of hunger and desire. It is the experience of being filled with the enjoyment of His abiding presence. It is more than yearning – it is consummation. He made us to go beyond our hunger to actually *taste* Him. That is why Psalm 34:8 invites those who are spiritually hungry to *"taste and see that the Lord is good."* Emotions are *not* the enemy of the believer. Dispassionate rule-keeping is! It is not wrong to seek to know God with our emotions and to seek the taste of *the kisses of His mouth.*

The Power of a Kiss

Kissing has been the subject and inspiration for every form of artistic expression from antiquity to the present time. It is the most common and universal way people express their love and affection. In addition to the pleasure it brings, a kiss also transmits a variety of biological and psychological signals affecting how two people perceive each other. Scientific studies suggest that when people kiss they may even detect the chemical information about the other person on a subconscious level. Our bodies produce "pleasure" pheromones when we kiss which actually alter our state of consciousness. Prolonged, passionate kissing can literally bring a person "under the influence" by inducing a kind of romantic intoxication. Studies have also shown that kissing can prevent the formation of certain harmful stress hormones. The effect can actually decrease the ill effects of high blood pressure,

---

[182] Matthew 5:6 NIV

decrease facial wrinkles, accelerate weight loss, sedate pain, mitigate depression, boost the immune system and even fight tooth decay! Indeed, a kiss is a powerful thing![183]

The bride in the *Song of Songs* begins her quest for love with a bold cry for deep affection. She dreams of what the kisses of her king might taste like. Her yearning is not for the kind of platonic kisses that pass between friends or even a romantic kiss placed gently upon the lips. *No!* She is very specific when she says that her desire is for "the kisses of his *mouth.*" The Hebrew word is *peh* and it refers to the "open mouth." Hers is a longing for a deep, open, intimate kiss.

The Transcendent Kiss

Paula Rinehart, in her book *Sex and the Soul of a Woman,*[184] likens sexuality and spirituality to two bookends of a person's life. Each feeds into the other because both spring from the same desire to find our significance and worth in the eyes of someone who looks upon us with love, acceptance, and desire. In regard to our *sexuality,* that person is meant to be our marriage partner. In regard to our *spirituality,* that person is *God.* Yet, how do we comprehend the kiss of God upon the soul of man? How do we experience intimacy with Christ? This is the crux of controversy regarding Bridal Theology. If being the Bride of Christ is our true identity and not merely a spiritualized metaphor, then what is the nature of the kiss we hunger for? I have been asked on more than one occasion if I am suggesting or encouraging people to somehow "have sex with Jesus." The first time I was asked that question I am sure my jaw dropped to the floor. You have to

---

[183] See an article titled "What's So Great About Kissing?" by Jeanie Lerche Davis at www.Webmd.com.

[184] Paula Rinehart, *Sex and the Soul of a Woman* (Grand Rapids: Zondervan, 2004)

admire people who cut through the clutter to get to the point. That question has caused me to ponder the logical end of my developing beliefs.

The Flame of Jah

The *Song* presents God as a deeply romantic lover who artfully woos His Bride with loving words of admiration and even playful allure. Almost every verse of the book drips with the thrill and beauty of romance. Although much of the *Song* is a simple dialogue between two lovers, it should be noted that the Shulamite was not the co-author of the book. Her words and the expression of her heart were written for her by Solomon. He wrote as one who knew the one he loved so well as to be acquainted with her deepest longings. King David said that God was "acquainted with all [his] ways,"[185] and our Bridegroom knows everything about us as well. He is qualified to be the "author and finisher of our faith"[186] because, as the Psalmist said:

> ...there is not a word on my tongue, but, Behold, O LORD, You know it altogether.[187]

It was Saint Augustine who said, "God is more intimate to me than I am to myself."

Perhaps a month after I began my own study of the *Song*, I noticed I was growing frustrated in not being able to clearly draw a theological context for the *Song*. Instead of theology, the book seemed to offer me nothing but *romance!* As I turned the pages of the book, I found myself drawn into a story that read more like a romance novel than a theological treatise. It described the tummy-

---

[185] Psalm 139:3
[186] Hebrews 12:2
[187] Psalm 139:4

flipping excitement characteristic of love in its early stages and showed how a relationship can mature from the point of giddy infatuation to deep, covenant love. But beyond that, I struggled to find solid theology in the book. It wasn't until I began to see that the romance itself *is the theology* that the book began to make sense to me. I believe God gave the *Song* to mankind because He wants us to see that at the very heart of all that we call doctrine and theology - there is romance. God not only loves us; He also *desires* us!

In the final chapter of the *Song*, the love between Solomon and his bride has deepened into something so powerful it is described as "a most vehement flame."[188] In the Hebrew language, the use of this phrase is more literally translated "a flame of ***Jah.***"[189] The actual Hebrew word is "schalhevet-jah." The ***Jah*** at the end of the word is a form of the name Yahweh. This is the one and only time a reference to God is made in the whole of the book. This is, in fact, the "discovery moment" of the whole book! Suddenly, we are made aware that all of the love, all of the drama, and all of the passion that we have read about in the *Song* is more than a human love story. It is a picture of the transcendent love that God has for His own Bride! It is really a picture of the "flame of Jah." It is the essence of God's own nature that emanates toward His Bride and is demonstrated as the sacred kiss she desires.

A Kiss is Still a Kiss

What, then, is the nature of this holy kiss? Depending on whom you ask, you might get several different answers. Historically, the longing for the kiss represents the longing of the Jews for their Messiah. Some say the kiss is the sum total of our salvation experience. Still others say it is the cry of the heart for a

---

[188] Song of Songs 8:6
[189] Young's Literal Translation of the Bible

deeper experience of communion with Christ. Most teach that the kiss is merely a metaphor for the Word of God. Few, however, are bold enough to presume that it might be exactly what it claims to be - *a kiss!* I think the inclination to spiritualize *The Kiss* into something metaphoric gives evidence to just how uncomfortable we are with issues of intimacy. The image of God as our benevolent benefactor suits us well. To imagine Him as a romantic God is less acceptable mainly because it seems to *sexualize* Him. However, it begs the question as to *why* God has chosen to present Himself in the role of the Bridegroom and *why* an event called the "Marriage of the Lamb" is part of His eternal plan? In ancient times, after the bridegroom and his bride had consummated their marriage, the bridegroom would remove the covering from their bed and present it to the wedding party so that the physical blood evidence of the bride's virginity could be seen and celebrated. While this seems strange to us today, it points to the importance of bringing the betrothal covenant to its natural fulfillment. Without consummation, the covenant could not really be sealed and finalized. What would we think of a new bridegroom who expressed no desire to make love to his bride? Would we not think he was dysfunctional? But, we readily accept the notion of an impotent and dispassionate Christ because to envision Him otherwise makes *us* uncomfortable. I would suggest that the desire to make Christ into a eunuch is evidence of our own dysfunction - *not His.*

In her commentary on the *Song of Songs* published in 1916, Cora Harris MacIlravy says this about the kiss:

> "The "kisses of the mouth," is the symbol of the close relation that is between a bride and a bridegroom. There may be kisses upon the hand, signifying respect and friendship; but the mouth is kept by the bride for the

bridegroom, and the bridegroom keeps these kisses for his bride. Here it is a token of the highest, closest communion and relation that one can have with the Lord. She is longing for the kiss of betrothal, which will be an earnest from Him that she is to be His bride. Who can tell the joy of those who approach close enough to receive the kiss, which is the seal of the closer relation with the Lord!"[190]

The Kiss from Twisted Lips

Brennan Manning, in his book *Ragamuffin Gospel,*[191] describes a tender scene that occurred between a young woman and her husband in a hospital room. To remove a tumor from the woman's cheek, her doctor had to cut a nerve in her face, causing her mouth to become twisted in palsy. Standing in the shadows of the dimly lit room, the doctor watched as the husband spoke tenderly to his wife after the surgery. "I like it. It's kind of cute," he said, commenting on her disfigured smile. Then he bent down, kissed her and conformed his lips to accommodate hers. Indeed, Jesus bent down from Heaven and expressed His love to a world full of people disfigured by sin by conforming Himself to *us* and kissing us tenderly with the kiss of His mouth.

Like the old hymn says:

Grace and love like mighty rivers
poured incessant from above
and heaven's peace and perfect justice
kissed a guilty world in love[192]

---

[190] Cora Harris MacIlravy, Christ and His Bride: An Exposition of the Song of Solomon, (Chicago, IL: El Bethel Publishing House,1916)
[191] Brennan Manning, *Ragamuffin Gospel* (Multnoma Publishing 1990, 2000)
[192] William Rees, *Here Is Love Vast as the Ocean* (Abingdon Press 18)

When God created the world, He did so by speaking things into existence. There was no personal touch involved. But when it came to man, He bent down low to the earth and lovingly formed Adam with His own hands. Then He drew even closer and touched His lips to the lips of the man He had made. God kissed man *"and Adam became a living soul."*[193]

The Uncomfortable Question

Let's return to the "uncomfortable question" as to whether or not Bridal Theology is about "having sex with Jesus." While I would prefer to be able to offer a simple and definitive "no" to that question, it would not provide a full and adequate answer. Certainly, when I speak of experiencing the affections of Jesus as our Bridegroom, I am definitely *not* referring to a kind of relationship that involves some sort of physical sexual union with Him. Nevertheless, I do believe without a doubt that the way God designed human love to be expressed intimately and sexually in marriage is a window of revelation into a more transcendent kind of spiritual union that Christ offers His Beloved. We cannot fail to see the significance of the fact that, after God created the first man and woman as reflections of His own image, His first command to them was to engage each other sexually.[194] Their intimate love was meant to be an expression of the creative love and power of God. The uncomfortable question, in my opinion, is much broader and deserving of more contemplation than a simple answer can afford. What, for example, *is* the scriptural significance of the Bridegroom and the Bride? Why has God chosen this particular image as a way of revealing Himself to us? Is the Marriage of the Lamb an actual event? If so, how *will* our wedding to Jesus be consummated? Why did God arrange for an erotic poem like the

---

[193] Genesis 2:7 KJV
[194] [28] Genesis1:28 contains the Edenic command to "be fruitful, and multiply."

Song of Songs to be included in the Bible? If we are designed in the image of God, does God possess something akin to human sexuality or is He an *asexual* Being? If sexuality is indeed a missing element in God's own nature, then why did He create us to be so *unlike* Himself in that one respect? Do these images present a Kingdom reality, or are they just complex metaphors? As you can see, in light of these many questions, a simple answer to the "uncomfortable question" will not suffice.

Comfortable with Intimacy

Until Jesus came, the Jews believed God was unapproachable. To them, He was Creator, Lawgiver, Deliverer and Righteous Judge. They dared not audibly speak the name of God or even write it for fear of making Him too personal. Jesus, on the other hand, talked about God in a way that brought Him *uncomfortably* close! He called God "Father," and this so infuriated the hyper-religious Jews of His day that they accused Him of the crime of blasphemy. He even called God "Abba,"[195] which is a term as personal as our word "daddy" or "papa." Jesus introduced a level of intimacy with the Father that the Jews could not accept. The revelation of Jesus as our Bridegroom is just as unacceptable or perhaps even more so for many people today. When we feel we must make *The Kiss* a mere metaphor rather than an actual experience of spiritual affection, it reveals our own discomfort with issues of intimacy or else our fear of man's opinion. Speaking personally, I did not arrive at the answer to this question by pursuing the *meaning* of *The Kiss* intellectually. I arrived at the answer *by being kissed.*

---

[195] Mark 14:36

Degrees of Intimacy

Have you noticed that some Christians seem to experience a much closer intimacy with God than others? There are a myriad of variables which relate to why this is so, but the main reason some people struggle with the thought of knowing God intimately is that they are uncomfortable with intimacy itself. The Bible says: "deep calls unto deep."[196] This means the depth and degree to which we are willing to allow God to know *us* is the same depth and degree to which He will allow us to know *Him*. Of course, God already knows us to the marrow of our bones. There is nothing about us that is hidden from His sight. Every hair on our head has been counted and catalogued. Nevertheless, we still hide from Him! Allowing Him to *know* the depths of who we are really means to allow Him access to the protected places of our hearts. We allow God to *know* us when we remove the fig leaf of shame and accept His love in the light and knowledge of our imperfections rather than in their concealment. In teaching on intimacy with God, I often tell people that each degree of intimacy that transpires between a man and his wife is marked by the removal of layers of clothing until at last both are completely naked. The more we intimately give ourselves to another, the more our imperfections can be seen. Those who possess a more intimate experience of the love of God are those who have incrementally drawn closer to Him by removing the layers of shame that cover their hearts. The deepest intimacy with God is celebrated when we return to that Edenic place where we are free to be transparently naked before Him, yet unashamed.[197]

---

[196] Psalm 42:7
[197] "Naked" in a metaphoric sense.

The Intimacy of Servants, Friends, Sons and Brides

The degree of intimacy we can enjoy with God is also dictated by how we conceive of ourselves in relation to Him. If, for example, we conceive of Him as our Master and ourselves as His servants, He will relate to us to that degree. It is not His perfect plan for us, but He will accommodate us at whatever level we are able to comprehend Him. Some have learned that they can be a friend of God while others have come into the deeper revelation of their status as sons of God. The deepest degree of intimacy with God, however, is bridal intimacy.

- A servant *prepares* the bed of his Master
- A friend may *sit upon* the bed of his friend
- A son may *sleep* in the bed of his father
- A bride's bed is a bed of *intimate communion*

Defining What it is We Want

Have you ever really thought about what it is you want from God? What is your expectation in living the Christian life? Is it health, wealth and a more prosperous standard of living you hope to obtain by learning to live according to the principles of God's Word? Are you seeking answers to the difficulties life has brought your way? Are you hoping God will make you a better person or heal your broken heart? When you pray, do you mainly ask for *things,* or does your heart pine for God Himself?

When I began to pour myself into the *Song of Songs,* I found that it began to pour itself into me! I discovered a powerful, bold and exciting revelation of the love of Christ. My sabbatical, which was originally scheduled to last only a few weeks, soon turned to months and eventually became a year. During that year, as I gave myself to an exhaustive study of the *Song,* I also experienced a total revolution of my prayer life. A deep longing began to grow in my heart to actually *experience* the kind of close, intimate communion with Christ that I was reading about in the Scriptures. Perhaps for the first time in my Christian life, I was able to define what it was I really wanted from God. If there was a *kiss* to be experienced - *I wanted it!*

My prayer life began to change. Gone was my "agenda driven" prayer list. Gone were my attempts to engage God into the affairs of *my* world. Now, I wanted Him to engage me into the affairs of *His.* Words became rare in those days as I sat in silence and allowed my heart to simply yearn to be kissed. I learned there is more value to be found in learning how to wait upon God than there is in trying to feverishly serve Him. Nothing else would satisfy my heart short of a true experience with Him and that is when I realized that I had defined it at last. What I *wanted* more than anything else was for God to want *me* more than anything else! That is what *The Kiss* is all about. The Shulamite describes her lover in this way:

> The voice of my beloved! Behold, he comes, leaping upon the mountains, bounding over the hills. My beloved is like a gazelle, or a young stag. Behold, there he stands behind our wall, gazing in at the windows, looking through the lattice.[198]

With all that the Church can offer us in the form of programs and support, what we truly crave is for God to leap over the wall of our intellect, ravish our senses and leave us faint with love! The Christian life is more than putting biblical principles to work in our lives. It is the passionate response of our heart to the call of our Bridegroom to join Him in the love story of all ages!

---

[198] Song of Songs 2:8-9 RSV

Prepare to be Ravished

William Blake wrote, *"Those who restrain desire do so because their desire is weak enough to be restrained."*[199]

People in love are rarely able to restrain their desire. In fact, they are often ruled by it! They are led about by their emotions and blinded to all that is sensible. Do not think that the kiss of God upon your soul will sharpen your intellect. Passion does not sharpen the mind - *it makes it dull!* That is why the bride in the *Song* describes herself as being "lovesick."[200] Do you really want *The Kiss*? Then prepare to be undone! Desire does not adhere to the demands of logical thinking - it wreaks havoc upon it! Love has the power to make a person deaf, dumb and blind to all reason. But with all the pitfalls, it is *oh so glorious to be in love!*

Sadly, there *are* those whose desire is weak enough to be restrained. It is restrained by the fear of what others will think or perhaps by the need to protect their reputation. There are those, however, whose desire and need for the love of Christ is so strong it compels them to press beyond their personal fears and the acceptable status quo of passionless religion to experience the affections of their Bridegroom God. Like the Shulamite, they are not content to live with anything less than to rest in the arms of their King and taste the passionate kisses of His mouth.

Holy Havoc

On Labor Day, 1995, our church experienced a dramatic and powerful outpouring of the Holy Spirit. God dropped down into our meeting that Sunday and made a complete mess of all our

---

[199] William Blake, The Marriage of Heaven and Hell (1790)
[200] Song of Songs 2:5

plans and programs. Our service, which normally lasted an hour and a half, ended up lasting *seven hours*! And even then, few people wanted to leave. After over a decade, that same outpouring continues today, although it is felt with more intensity at some times and less at others. In the first few months of the outpouring, however, a local pastor who had attended some of our meetings contacted me. He wanted to know how his church might experience the same kind of visitation of the Spirit. He said he was looking for something that would get people excited and involved in the programs of his church once again. I hated to tell him, but when God decides to manifest His power and presence in a place He doesn't do so just to *enhance* what we are already doing. His presence tends to wreck all our programs! After all, who wants to be in a classroom studying *about* God when they can actually *be* with God?

I am a firm believer that one kiss *from* God can achieve more than a thousand sermons *about* God and, while certainly not a theologian, I think Shakespeare got it right when he spoke of a kiss that was so powerful *"all the church did echo!"*

12

BECOMING THE BELOVED

Who is this that cometh up from the wilderness,
leaning upon her beloved?
Song of Songs 8:5

Transformed By Love

It has been said that God loves us just the way we are and He also loves us too much to let us *stay* the way we are. The Shulamite began her journey in the first chapter of the *Song* as one unaware of her own true worth. Her heart had to be awakened to the truth of the value and beauty she possessed. The Shulamite's transformation was the result of the way her King patiently and persistently lavished her with complimentary words of love and acceptance. He did not tell her *once* that he loved her; he expressed his love and desire for her at every possible opportunity. So it is with you and me. Our salvation came in the blink of an eye. The time it takes for our hearts to be healed and transformed, however, depends on our ability to receive and respond to the love that Christ offers us. Knowing - *really knowing* - that God loves us is the basis for all true spirituality. If we live with no conscious awareness of His love, then His love can produce nothing in us.

In the first chapter of the *Song*, the Shulamite cries out for her Beloved to draw her to himself. She says, "Draw me and we will run together!"[201] Solomon's first reply to her, however, seems a strange one indeed. He says to her,

> I have compared you, my love, to my filly among Pharaoh's chariots.[202]

Pharaoh, of course, represents bondage to sin. Although she wanted to run with her Beloved, she was ill-equipped to do so as long as she was still harnessed to her old life. But in the final chapter of the *Song*, the Shulamite is portrayed as one emerging from the wilderness "leaning upon her Beloved." She was transformed at last!

Healed by a Kiss

Once I was teaching a series of messages from the *Song of Songs* in the United Kingdom. I had taught a session on the verse "kiss me with the kisses of your mouth" in the evening, and the next morning a woman asked if she could share something. With tears, she told of a childhood filled with sexual abuse and exploitation. As a young woman, she had thrown herself into a lifestyle of drugs, alcohol and promiscuity in an attempt to escape her pain. She told of how she eventually came to know the Lord and also how she had met and married a wonderful Christian man. Shortly after they were married, however, she discovered that she had an aversion to being kissed on the lips. She knew it was because she felt a deep shame for her past sins. Yet, even though she knew the source of her dysfunction, when her husband tried to kiss her, she would recoil and even become physically ill. This had been the story of their marriage for twenty years! While her husband had adjusted to her problem, their

[201] Song of Songs 1:4 Author's paraphrase
[202] Song of Songs 1:9

intimate relationship had suffered greatly. She had listened as I told the story of how the Shulamite's life had been transformed by the loving words of her King and the kiss of his mouth. That evening, she went home and fell asleep asking God to heal her with His kiss. The next morning, as her husband was leaving for work, he bent down to kiss her goodbye on the forehead. As he did, she opened her eyes, put her arms around his neck and drew his lips to hers. As they kissed, she felt a sense of her own worth and value flooding into her soul.

After giving her testimony she added, "I would love to stay and hear the next message, but my husband is coming home for lunch and I promised to be there when he arrived." We all laughed and rejoiced with her as she shot out of the door. She had a lot of missed kisses to catch up on!

You Are Worth It All

True love is *a reckless, passionate pursuit.* As Robert Frost put it, *"Love is the irresistible desire to be irresistibly desired."* In the sixth chapter of the *Song of Songs,* Solomon makes the following statement to his bride:

> Turn your eyes away from me, For they have confused me.[203]

Imagine, if you can, that when Jesus looks at you, He is mesmerized by your beauty. He is overcome and even confused by your presence. It's difficult for some people to imagine God's mind becoming clouded with love. They imagine that God's hand is always on the control panel of the universe and that He is never distracted from running every minute detail of the cosmos. If you

---

[203] Song of Solomon 6:5 NAS

imagine that God is primarily the *manager* of the universe, then the image of Him made giddy by love is a frightening one indeed. What would happen if He should become momentarily distracted from His duties? Would the world shift on its axis? Would the heavens roll up like a scroll? Consider how risky it was for Jesus to leave heaven and come to earth in the form of a helpless baby. He made Himself totally dependent on others to care for His every need and keep Him safe. Just think - His parents left Him behind in Jerusalem when He was just a child! How dangerous was that? Nevertheless, in the days when God made Himself into a weak and fragile human being, the universe still clicked along with no problems. So I have no problem believing that God can simultaneously run the universe with meticulous precision while at the same time being absolutely love-struck by the mere sight of me (and you!). *I firmly believe that God is a capable "multi-tasker"!*

Gazing Upon God with Eyes of Love

If gazing at the beauty of redeemed man can confound the mind of God, what must it do to the mind of man to gaze back into the perfect beauty of all that God is? I had a personal experience several years ago in which I was given just a brief glimpse into what can only be described as the beauty realm of the Lord. I remember how suddenly my thoughts seemed to melt into unintelligible gibberish as I gazed into a domain beyond this world. I came away from that experience with a keen appreciation and understanding of what the Apostle Paul meant when he said it was inappropriate for him to speak of the things he had witnessed in the third heaven.[204] I admit that I am highly suspect of those who freely share in great detail about their own "angelic encounters" and "third heaven experiences." It's not that I don't believe people have such encounters - *I do.* It's just that I have

---

[204] 2 Corinthians 12:2

learned from experience that when God makes a person privy to such knowledge, it is too wonderful and too intimate to share with a wide audience. After the angel Gabriel appeared to Mary and told her about the miracle that was growing in her womb, she didn't try to use her experience as a platform upon which to build a ministry. Instead, the Bible tells us that she "kept all these things, and ***pondered*** them in her heart."[205] Despite the grandiose stories told by those whose credibility in ministry is literally built upon such tales, those who truly seek to gaze into the eyes of Jesus actually run the risk of having their ministries dismantled before their very eyes! When Isaiah, whose ministry was already well established, looked beyond the veil and into the eyes of God, the experience left him exclaiming, "I am undone!"[206]

David's Vision of a Royal Wedding

As shown in a previous chapter, Psalm 45 is a prophetic vision King David had concerning the wedding of Solomon. It begins with what appears to be a description of David sending his son to war.

> Gird thy sword upon thy thigh, O most mighty, with thy glory and thy majesty. And in thy majesty ride. [207]

Abruptly, however, the scene changes from what seemed like a war to a wedding! David continues,

> …upon thy right hand did stand the queen [bride] in gold of Ophir…She shall be brought unto the king in raiment of

---

[205] Luke 2:19 KJV
[206] Isaiah 6:5
[207] Psalm 45:3 KJV

> needlework: the virgins her companions[208] that follow her shall be brought unto thee. With gladness and rejoicing shall they be brought: they shall enter into the king's palace.[209]

An understanding of this ancient Jewish wedding custom adds comprehension to these verses. You will recall that when the wedding finally arrived, the bridegroom secretly gathered his wedding party and made a joyful procession to the bride's home. He would ride upon a wooden platform carried upon the shoulders of the men of the wedding entourage. This procession was actually a drama in which the bridegroom played the part of a conquering king. Before leaving his home, his father placed a garland upon his head to represent his kingly crown. The men in his wedding party escorted him along the path as his personal army. He, along with all the other men, would gird real swords upon their thighs. Once the wedding party drew close to their destination, the bride would come out to meet her bridegroom in the street. Then they would return in recession to his father's house where the ceremony would take place.

Do you see the significance? When Jesus made His way to Golgotha, it was actually *His* wedding procession! He went to the Cross to receive His Bride! The crown of thorns upon His head was, in a paradoxical way, His wedding garland. The Roman soldiers who escorted Jesus to the Cross with their swords strapped to their thighs unwittingly played the part of His wedding party. In the beautiful language of the *Song of Songs* the Crucifixion of Jesus is ironically referred to as His *wedding day.*

> Go forth, O ye daughters of Zion, and behold King

[208] The "virgin companions" of the bride in Psalm 45 are synonymous to the "Daughters of Jerusalem" depicted in the *Song of Songs*.
[209] Psalm 45:9,14 KJV

> Solomon with the crown wherewith his mother crowned him in the day of his **espousals**, and in the day of the gladness of his heart.[210] [emphasis added]

Notice it was Solomon's *mother* who placed his wedding garland upon his head. Since by tradition this was done by the father, this indicates that David had probably died by this time. As a figure of Christ, it was fitting that Solomon would receive His wedding crown from his mother because Jesus received His wedding crown of thorns at the hand of His *spiritual* mother, Israel. Bathsheba's name means "she who takes an oath" and you will remember that when Pilate sought to release Jesus, the crowd of Jews gathered at his palace and cried out for a notorious criminal named Barabbas to be released instead. And in so doing, they took this **oath** upon themselves:

> [Let] His blood be on us, and on our children.[211]

I don't mean to imply that the Jews were the only ones who were complicit in the death of Christ. The Romans were equally guilty. But ultimately, the death of Jesus was neither the result of the actions of the Jews nor the Romans. The Cross was a choice Jesus made *for Himself*. That choice is alluded to in the third chapter of the *Song of Songs*, where we find a dramatic picture of Solomon riding across the desert sands to collect his bride for her wedding.

> Who is this that cometh out of the wilderness like pillars of smoke, perfumed with myrrh and frankincense, with all powders of the merchant? Behold his bed, which is Solomon's; threescore valiant men are about it, of the

---

[210] Song of Songs 3:11 KJV
[211] Matthew 27:25

> valiant of Israel. They all hold swords, being expert in war: every man hath his sword upon his thigh because of fear in the night. *King Solomon made himself a chariot of the wood of Lebanon.* He made the pillars thereof of silver, the bottom thereof of gold, the covering of it of purple, the midst thereof being paved with love, for the daughters of Jerusalem.[212] [emphasis added]

The word "chariot" in this verse is the word *aperion* (אפריון) which, as I have already explained, was a wooden platform upon which the bridegroom traveled to his wedding. This is the "bed" upon which Solomon rode. It is intriguing that Solomon is identified as the one who built his own aperion. Why would a king perform this kind of manual labor when skilled craftsmen were at his disposal? To answer this question, we have to look at the rich symbolism of these verses. Wood, in the Bible, often represents the Cross of Christ. Although pure speculation, it is entirely possible that Jesus, being a carpenter, made the very cross upon which He was crucified. Even if He did not, the Cross was still clearly something Christ "made for Himself" in the sense that He *chose* to lay down His life. We are told that the pillars of the aperion were made of silver, the seat was made of gold, and the canopy above was made of purple. Silver is the metal of redemption, gold the metal of divinity, and purple, the color of royalty. Christ, who was divinity (gold), went to the cross to secure redemption (silver) robed in purple (royalty).[213] Remember too that the wooden aperion was carried upon the shoulders of the bridegroom's friends. Was Christ's wooden aperion (the Cross) carried on the shoulders of another in fulfillment of the type? *The answer is a marvelous "yes!"*

---

[212] Song of Songs 3:6-10 KJV
[213] Mark 15:17

> Now as they came out, they found a man of Cyrene, Simon by name. *Him they compelled to bear His cross.*[214]

How complete in every detail is the story of God's salvation!

The Manifestation of the Bride

We should examine closely the lives of Abishag, Esther, Ruth, Rebecca, the Shulamite and the other brides of the Bible so that a composite picture of what it means to be the *Beloved* will begin to take shape in our understanding. These brides all comprise the one divine blueprint from which the reality of *the* spiritual Bride is being formed today. As in the life of each of these brides, a transformation was necessary before they were "made ready" for their kings. So it is with us today. God is calling us to change the way we view Him—and in so doing, the way we view ourselves. I believe the *Beloved* of Christ is already present in the world today and that an unparalleled love and passion for Jesus is growing in her heart. An experience of God's divine, romantic love has been sent from heaven as a fire upon the altar of those whose hearts hunger for the experience of God's intimate affections. Like Abishag, she has been called to leave the beggarly things of life behind and advance to royalty. Like the Shulamite, she has been called to know the intimate, sacred kiss of her Bridegroom King. Like Ruth, she has been called to lie at the feet of her Lord in humble devotion until He awakens to her deepest need to have a kinsman-redeemer. Like Esther, she has been called forth at a strategic time. Like Rebecca, the Bride is on her way to meet her Bridegroom at the "end of the day!"[215]

---

[214] Matthew 27:32

[215] Genesis 24:63 Isaac met Rebecca at "eventide" or at the last rays of the day's light - a picture of the end of time.

Without a doubt, the end of time will be a perilous time of spiritual darkness and even what the Bible calls "gross darkness."[216] But against the backdrop of this pervasive spiritual darkness, a bright revelation of God's love will shine one last time upon a fallen world before the end comes. The final revelation of God's great love for mankind will be lifted up against the floodwaters of cold love. Like an underwater volcano, it will burn against all resistance with "flashes of fire" until it culminates in what is called "a most vehement flame."[217] The Hebrew word for "vehement flame" is *shalhebeth* (תבהלש) meaning "the essence of Jehovah."

Beloved, before the Bride of Christ is taken from this world, she will demonstrate to the world the pure essence of the love of God. It is holy Bridal love born from true intimate encounters that will be the hallmark of this chosen, lovesick remnant of people.

The Surpassing Beauty of the Bride

In the fourth chapter of the *Song*, the Bridegroom praises the surpassing beauty of his Bride in painstaking detail. He speaks of the enchanting quality of her eyes, her hair, her lips and even her breasts. And then, as if stepping back to appraise the entirety of her beauty, he exclaims:

> [To have this woman] *"I will get me to the mountain of myrrh, and to the hill of frankincense.*[218]

The mountain of myrrh and the hill of frankincense is clearly an allusion to Golgotha. Myrrh is a reddish resin

---

[216] Isaiah 60:2
[217] Song of Songs 8:6
[218] Song of Songs 4:1-6 KJV

reminiscent of human blood and means "suffering and death." Frankincense was a spice that was sprinkled upon the flesh of every sacrifice offered in the Temple. When burned, it produced a sweet white smoke and represented the pure sinless offering that was the body of Christ. The verse that follows says,

"Thou art all fair, my love; there is no spot in thee."[219]

There is a glorious freedom that comes in knowing - *really knowing* - that the Cross worked! Because of what Christ accomplished on the mountain of myrrh and the hill of frankincense, we have been made forever spotless, accepted and utterly desirable to God! He can never love you more for your achievements, nor will He ever love you less for your failures.

My Personal Struggle

For most of my Christian life, I was not truly convinced of the power of the Cross. I believed it mentally but not experientially. I could preach sermons about the perfect work of the Cross while at the same time alternating between feelings of being absolutely loved by God one day and being barely *liked* by Him the next. The sense of my own frail humanity was more real to me than the power of God's love. Despite what I knew about the love of God doctrinally, I never felt passionately loved and desired by Him. If anything, I felt dutifully *tolerated* by God. That all changed when God began to reveal to me my own true identity as His *Beloved*. As I pondered the words of the *Song of Songs*, I saw that the Shulamite bride was actually a revelation of my own heart. Her greatest struggle, like my own, was coming to the place where she actually *believed* the words of her king when he told her of his love and desire for her. When I began to think of myself in

[219] Song of Songs 4:7 KJV

spiritually feminine terms, I discovered the key to experiencing the intimate, relationship with Christ I sought. The Christian author, C. S. Lewis, once remarked that *"God is so masculine, we are all feminine in comparison!"* Knowing Christ in His identity as my Bridegroom granted me a sense of my own true identity as well. I came to understand that being His Bride had nothing to do with my gender or marital status. *Being His Bride is a state of heart.*

The Meaning of Life

I labored for many years under the assumption that I had been *"saved to serve"* God. I wanted to please Him, therefore I sought to know what it was He expected of me. Often, as a pastor, I have had people say to me, "If I only knew what God wanted, I would do it." In the final analysis, God does not really need for you and me to *do* anything for Him. What God really *needs* and *wants* is us! I was created to be the "feminine" side of the marriage covenant with Christ! As the reality of this revelation took root in my heart and mind, I began to see that the reason I was created was for the same reason Eve was created - *to meet a need in the heart of my Husband.* The Westminster Confession states that *"man's chief end is to glorify God, and to enjoy Him forever."* If I had the power to do so, I would add to that confession the words *"and to be enjoyed by Him forever."*

Of Husbands and Wives

In light of this, consider carefully what the Bible tells us about marriage because it is the blueprint of our relationship with Christ. God tells husbands to "love [their] wives, and be not bitter against them."[220] The word "bitter" means to "treat with anger or

[220] Colossians 3:19

exasperation." If Christ expects *earthly husbands* to treat their wives with gentleness and patience, then as the Bride of Christ, I can fully expect the same consideration and attitude from Him toward me. In the book of Ephesians we are told that "no one ever hated his own flesh; but nourishes and cherishes it, just as the Lord does the church."[221] There are so many times when I have hated my own flesh and its appetite for sin. Yet Christ has willingly joined Himself to the weakness of my flesh! He has even gone so far as to make Himself "one flesh" with me![222] Truly, He has married us for "better or worse" and often He is the recipient of the *worst* of us and not the best. Yet, His love for us is so great and His heart so tender He is willing to be identified with the weakest and worst part of us - *our flesh*. In the book of 1 Peter, a similar thought is presented when husbands are told to give honor to their wives as the *weaker partner* in the marriage.[223] This means that Christ understands that you and I are weak in regard to our human nature and that despite our best efforts and intentions, sin sometimes dominates our desires. When that happens, Christ does not reject us or divorce us. He patiently nurtures us back to proper relationship. He is the stronger partner and does not hold our weaker condition against us.

King David wrote:

> The LORD is merciful and gracious, slow to anger and abounding in steadfast love. He will not always chide, nor will He keep his anger forever. He does not deal with us according to our sins, nor requite us according to our iniquities. For as the heavens are high above the earth, so great is His steadfast love toward those who fear Him; as

---

[221] Ephesians 5:29
[222] Ephesians 5:31
[223] 1 Peter 3:7

> far as the east is from the west, so far does He remove our transgressions from us. As a father pities his children, so the LORD pities those who fear Him. For He knows our frame; He remembers that we are dust. As for man, his days are like grass; he flourishes like a flower of the field; for the wind passes over it, and it is gone, and its place knows it no more. But the steadfast love of the LORD is from everlasting to everlasting upon those who fear Him…[224] [emphasis added]

How comforting to know that God does not expect us to be *God!* He is mindful of the frailty of our nature. He knows that we are the "weaker vessel" and remembers that we are only made of dust. He does not deal with us according to our sins, otherwise we would have no hope. Instead He deals with us from the standpoint of the abundance of His loving-kindness and the multitude of His tender mercies!

Wives Be Submissive

The Bridal revelation revolutionized my very concept of God and in the process revolutionized my prayer life as well. Like many people, prayer had always been a constant struggle. I approached prayer as a necessary, yet unappealing part, of the Christian life. The models of prayer I witnessed led me to believe that effective praying was *assertive* praying. When I prayed, I felt it was up to me to "rend the heavens and go up" rather than for God to "rend the heavens and come down."[225] I would often engage in what is commonly called "spiritual warfare" as I would wrestle and strive in an effort to obtain a "breakthrough." I would often emerge from such prayer feeling uncertain that anything had

[224] Psalm 103:8-17 RSV
[225] Isaiah 64:1

really been accomplished. There are times when it is not only appropriate, but also absolutely necessary to become aggressive and assertive in prayer. But prayer is not only about obtaining something or making something happen; it is also very much about experiencing God's intimate love. As the "feminine" Bride, I began to see that my role in prayer was primarily to become submissive rather than assertive toward Christ, my Husband.[226] The word "submissive" is the Greek word *hypotassō* (ὑποτάσσω) and speaks primarily of a person's physical position. Literally, it means to "come up under" or to "have something placed on top of you."

Notice that when Paul teaches about how husbands and wives should relate to each other in the fifth chapter of Ephesians, he admonishes husbands to love, cherish, nourish and protect their wives to the point of defending them to the death, if needed. And then he tells wives to respond to their husbands by becoming *submissive* to their husband's cherishing love. In other words, Paul was telling them to position themselves to become *receivers* of love! Those who have told women that their duty was to be happily dominated and even abused by their husbands have failed to grasp the real meaning of what the Bible says. Paul used the analogy of marriage as a way of expressing the more profound quality of the love of Christ. In no way is Jesus a domineering or abusive husband!

A Receptacle for Love

Physiologically, a woman's body is designed to be the *receptacle* of her husband's love. She was created by God to take her husband *into* herself through the act of lovemaking. In the same way, our heart is not made to *initiate* love toward God. Our

[226] Ephesians 5:22

soul is designed to *receive* the love of God; and in the receiving of God's love, we are enabled to return our love to Him.

> We love Him, because He **first loved us.**[227] [emphasis added]

When I came to understand this important principle, I found that prayer finally became the source of delight and pleasure I had always hoped it would be.

The Glory of God

One of the most interesting words in the Hebrew language is the word "glory." It is the word *kabod* (דבכ) and it means "a weight that is felt." I am convinced that God not only wants us to know that we are loved theologically, but He also wants us to *feel* the affections of His love. There are many ways in which a wife can know the presence of her husband. She can know his presence if she hears his voice nearby. She can even recall his presence merely by smelling his cologne. In the *Song,* the bride recalls Solomon's presence as the fragrance of sweet myrrh.

> My beloved is to me a bag of myrrh, that lies between my breasts.[228]

Of all the ways a wife can know her husband's presence, there is only one time when she feels his presence as a *felt weight,* and that is when they make love. Likewise there are foretastes of the glory and Presence of Christ to be found in the place of intimate prayer.

---

[227] 1 John 4:19
[228] Song of Songs 1:13 RSV

The Ark of the Covenant

Like most people, I was taught that the Ark of the Covenant was a representation of God on earth. *It is not.* Basically, the Ark of the Covenant was a wooden box overlaid with gold. It was a repository for the tablets of the Law, a pot of manna, and Aaron's rod that budded. The Ark is a representation of the spirit of man, and more specifically, a representation of the Bride of Christ. Gold overlaid on wood is a picture of God's immortal nature covering the perishable nature of man. The Ark was the resting place for the Presence of God. It was the one place on earth where God laid the intimate weight of His *kabod* and therefore it serves as a picture of divine intimacy. The more intimate a relationship becomes, the more need there is for privacy. For this reason, the inner sanctum of the Holy of Holies, which housed the Ark, was hidden from the gaze of human eyes by a thick curtain.

The Hidden Manna

One of the items concealed within the confines of the Ark was a jar containing manna. You will recall that in the Holy Place of the Temple there were twelve loaves of bread which were visible to the priests who ministered there on a daily basis. Those loaves were called the "shewbread" or "the Bread of the Presence." The shewbread represents Jesus who came to earth in the flesh and was made manifest to the world as the bread of life.[229] The manna *inside* the Ark is also a representation of Jesus; except in a form that is *not* readily visible. The manna inside the Ark was the "hidden manna" representing the indwelling presence of Jesus in the heart of every believer. Mickey McNew, in

[229] John 6:48

his book *You Are At The Time For Love,*[230] recalls a scene from the *Song of Songs* when Solomon appears to his bride. His hair is "drenched with the dew, and the dampness of the night."[231] Mickey points out that the manna which the Israelites ate in the wilderness appeared as "dew" on the ground each morning.[232] Jesus is the "hidden manna" that becomes manifest only to those who dare to go beyond the veil in search of intimate union with God. In the book of Revelation, Jesus promises to those who have an ear to hear that He will give them the right to eat the *hidden manna* of intimacy.[233]

The Call to Become

Becoming the Beloved is a call to a deeper, more intimate relationship with Jesus as our Bridegroom. I am convinced that the Bridal revelation only becomes a true reality in our lives when it translates into a joyful lifestyle of devoted prayer. When the Holy Spirit began to illumine some of the precious truths of the *Song of Songs* to me, it aroused a deep hunger in my heart to actually *know* the same kind of intimate affection that the Shulamite experienced with her King. I knew there had to be more to the Christian life than mere principles and precepts. No one in my Christian journey had ever explained to me what it meant to be "kissed with the kisses of His mouth." I had no point of reference as to what kind of expectation that should engender. I had no mentor and no teacher to guide me. All I possessed was the desire to be desired, and from there my journey began

[230] McNew, Mickey, You Are At The Time For Love, (Set Us Free Jesus Publishing ©2007, pg 89)
[231] Song of Songs 5:2 KJV
[232] Numbers 11:9
[233] Revelation 2:17

Jabez Who?

Several years ago, a best-selling book called *The Prayer of Jabez* hit the market like a windstorm. The author, Bruce Wilkinson, aptly tapped into something in the Body of Christ that turned the book into a literal phenomenon. Spin-offs of the book in various forms soon followed. In case you happen to be the one person in the world who has *not* read the book, I will give you a brief synopsis.

Jabez was a man in the Bible who prayed a simple prayer which consisted of four petitions. First, he asked God to bless him. Second, he asked God to enlarge his territory. Third, he prayed that God would be on his side and finally, he asked that God would keep him from experiencing pain. I believe the reason the book was such an amazing success is because it accurately reflects what the majority of people in the Church are seeking from God. Basically we just want to be blessed, be given more stuff to play with, and avoid pain at all costs. Despite the popularity of the book, this is perhaps the best example of how NOT to pray! What is often overlooked about Jabez and his prayer is that this is the one and only time Jabez is ever mentioned in the whole of the Word of God! He was a "one prayer wonder!" *He had no longevity in regard to destiny!* He would have remained an obscure, insignificant biblical figure if Bruce Wilkinson had not written the book. It is not those who seek mere blessing that find their destiny in God; it is those who pray, *"Show me your glory!"*

Life is not about accumulating more stuff or avoiding pain. Life is about finding our identity and significance in God. The bride in the *Song* does not cry out, "Give me, give me" - she prays, "Kiss me, kiss me!" The Bridal Revelation delivered me from what I call "agenda driven" or "need based" praying to what I now call "relationship prayer." Since God is my Husband, it is *His* responsibility and even His delight to care for my daily needs. The goal of prayer from beginning to end is to experience union and communion with Christ. When the Apostle Paul makes the analogy between the relationship of husbands and wives with Christ and His Church, he quotes a verse from Genesis which says:

> For this reason a man shall leave his father and mother and be joined to his wife, and the two shall become one flesh. This mystery is a profound one, and I am saying that it refers to Christ and the church. [234]

Christ is the One who left His Father's house to be joined to His wife! We need to understand that, while we might perceive that the ultimate goal of our salvation is to secure ourselves a place in Heaven, from Christ's perspective, the ultimate goal of our salvation is that He gets to be become "one" with us! And the way we become one with Christ is through the intimacy of communion. Therefore, my goal in prayer is to learn how to rest and receive my Bridegroom's love.

Entering the Rest of God

On the eve of the Sabbath, after all work has stopped and just before sunset, observant Jews begin the evening by lighting candles, saying prayers, pronouncing blessings, and singing traditional songs. Though not widely known, the Sabbath is called *"the welcoming of the bride"* by Jews. Everything that takes place around the Sabbath table reflects this idea. After the candles are lit, for instance, the father of the house sings a song to honor the bride. The song is called the *eshet chayil,* which means "woman of

---

[234] Ephesians 5:31-32 RSV

virtue." It comes from the book of Proverbs 31 in which the virtues of woman are extolled. The father also takes a silver cup called the "kiddush," fills it with wine and recites a traditional blessing. The kiddush cup is the same kind of ritual cup that is used to bring a man and woman into their betrothal covenant! In the Talmud *(which is a commentary of the Scriptures written by noted rabbis)*, the Sabbath is also personified as a beautiful bride who is to be greeted each week with celebration and joy. Because of this, the Sabbath is spoken of as a feminine "she," not an "it."

Challah Bread

The most striking symbolic picture of the Bride during the Sabbath celebration is the centerpiece of the table. It is a special loaf of bread called the *challah bread.* The challah bread is actually made by taking two separate loaves and twisting them together so that they are formed into what is called the "lover's embrace." In fact, the very word "challah" (הלכ) (pronounced *kal·lä'*) means "the bride!" Customarily, Jewish couples enter the rest of God each week by making love on Friday night.

It Is Finished

In the ancient Hebrew language, the same sounding words are sometimes used to convey different meanings much like the English words "deer" and "dear." The Hebrew word "challah" which refers to the Sabbath bread sounds exactly like the word "kallah" which means "to finish." They are written using the exact same characters which appear as הלכ. Although the New Testament manuscripts from which our Bibles are translated were written in Koine (or common) Greek, Jesus did not speak Greek. He would have spoken the language of His culture, which was a form of Hebrew known as Aramaic. The Gospel of John tells us that the last words of Jesus from the Cross were the words "it is finished" (Aramaic: *kallah*).[235] The words of Christ contained a deep and beautiful dual meaning. In one sense, Jesus was saying that by His death on the Cross the sin debt mankind owed was paid in full (finished.) In another sense, He was saying, "Finally, I will have My Bride! (kallah)"

[235] John 19:13

13

MAKING IT A REALITY

The soul that can speak through the eyes,
can also kiss with a gaze.
Gustav Adolfo Becquer

How Do We Make This A Reality?

Admiring the opposite sex does not make us married. Neither does admiring Christ as the Bridegroom avail us of what it means to be His Bride. The true relationship that affords us intimacy with Christ begins as a complete commitment of all that we are to Him. What does it mean to actually *Become The Beloved?* How can we make the Bridal revelation the real substance of our life? While it may be possible to lay a basic foundation for how to make it a reality, each of us must build upon that foundation in our own way. Seeking and finding God is a process unique to every person. Moses encountered God in a burning bush; Elijah, in a still small voice. Jonah "saw the light" in the dark belly of a great fish and King David found the Holy One while he was hiding for his life in the cave of Adullam. You will find Him as well, but it may come in a way you least expect.

Called and Chosen

I believe that God calls everyone to know Him personally and intimately. But while everyone may be called, not everyone will *choose to be chosen.* Jewish brides were never forced to marry the man selected for them. They always had the right of refusal, and so do we! We can choose or refuse to *Become the Beloved.* If you have caught a glimpse of the truth that Jesus is indeed not only *the* Bridegroom but *your* Bridegroom, then you are already face to face with the call to discover the fullness of this truth. Deep will ultimately call to deep as Saint Augustine's words express, *"My soul is restless until it rests in you, O God."*

Living Loved

Becoming the Beloved is more than an exalted idea of the kind of relationship which *might* be possible with God someday. We can make the decision right now to begin to *live loved.* We need not strive to *Become the Beloved* in the sense of making ourselves more presentable and desirable to God by good works. We *Become the Beloved* by simply receiving the love He offers us freely. When Christ called us and declared us to be His Bride, that and that alone became the validation of our worth. We may be immature and clumsy at living the Christian life, yet we can still *live loved* because it is *God's choice* to make us the object of His love - not our own. Do we deserve His love? *No.* Do we always live in a way that honors the love we've been shown? *We do not.* Should we expect God to continue to express His love to us when we fail Him continuously? *No.* But He does and that is His choice! God has chosen to love us, and the only choice He has left for us to make is whether or not we will receive the gift of His love.

Learning How to Live Loved

Living loved does not come to us easily because all of our lives we have been bombarded with the idea that we will only be loved if we are the most beautiful, the most intelligent, or the most successful we can be. When we have no sense of our own core value and worth to God, we will do whatever we think we must do in order to make ourselves loveable. Our feelings of being unloved can even drive us to grasp for love in ways that are unhealthy or sinful. The source of many relational problems is that we place unreasonable expectations on what people are able to give us. We look to others to make us ultimately happy and to love us unconditionally. The only person who has the ability to love unconditionally is God. Our best efforts at unconditional love are limited by our own humanity. At some point, we all selfishly demand our own way or put our interests first. All of our disappointing efforts to find authentic love and all of the false messages we have embraced as truth about God, ourselves, and others must change. We have to learn how to *live loved.* The Bible calls this learning process a transformation that comes by the *"renewing of our minds."* [236] The Greek word for "renewing" is the word *anakainōsis* (ἀνακαίνωσις). It's a word that came into use during the time following the birth of Christianity. The Jewish historian, Josephus,[237] uses the word to describe the restoration of the Jewish nation after the period of the Babylonian captivity. In that sense, *Becoming the Beloved* requires the rebuilding of the ruins of our distorted thinking so that our hearts and minds become a dwelling place for God's love and Presence.

Longing to be Loved

Oswald Chambers said, "Prayer is the way the life of God is nourished." Though not everyone is consciously aware of it, the basic drive of everyone's life is to find God, to worship Him, and to hear His voice. The genesis of our *Becoming the Beloved* is found in simple *longing.* The *Song of Songs* begins with the Shulamite

---

[236] Romans 12:2
[237] (Antiquities of the Jews, *Antt.* xi. 3. 9)

expressing her desire to be in a deeper relationship with her King; one which afforded her kisses. The alarming pervasiveness of substance abuse, sexual addiction and the grasping for power in our society is actually a symptom of the deeper unmet longing for the love of God in the human heart. The end result of such misplaced longing is idolatry. These misplaced longings are not only visible in society, but they also hide unseen in the hearts and minds of people of faith who, despite their love for God, still struggle to feel loved by Him. What we really long for is to be held close by God. The only thing that can satisfy that longing is an authentic relationship with God forged in prayer.

Learning to Listen

I am convinced that *listening* with the desire to hear the voice of God in prayer is more important than speaking to Him. Let's face it - everything about us is already known by God. There is nothing left to be revealed. In Psalm 139, David wrote about how God had searched his heart to the utter depths. Even the most mundane parts of David's life were known by God. He knew when David sat down and when he rose up. He even knew the very words David would speak while they were yet on his tongue. Beloved, more is known about us by God than we know about ourselves! On the other hand, practically *everything* about God remains a mystery to you and me. Prayer is an opportunity for God to reveal Himself to us.

Turning Down the Noise

Not everyone who hears truly listens. Jesus often called for those who "had ears to hear, to listen."[238] In any conversation, we

---

[238] Matthew 11:15

cannot hear the other person if we are talking or if our minds are distracted. So it is with listening for the voice of God. If we want to hear Him, we must turn down the noise, quiet ourselves, and focus on what He might say. Consider setting aside a quiet, undisturbed place where you can meet with God on a daily basis. We live in a noisy world where almost everywhere we go, other voices are competing for our attention. The devotion to intimate prayer is perhaps the crowning hallmark that distinguishes those who are the Bride of Christ.

Learning the Value of Solitude

Consider the way Jesus prayed:

> "And in the morning, a great while before day, He rose and went out to a lonely place, and there He prayed."[239] [emphasis added]

> "...great multitudes gathered to hear and to be healed of their infirmities. But He withdrew to the wilderness and prayed." [240] [emphasis added]

> "...He went out to the mountain to pray; and all night He continued in prayer to God."[241] [emphasis added]

> "And after He had dismissed the crowds, He went up on the mountain by Himself to pray. When evening came, He was there alone..." [242] [emphasis added]

---

[239] Mark 1:35 RSV
[240] Luke 5:15-16 RSV
[241] Luke 6:12 RSV
[242] Matthew 14:23 RSV

The habit of Jesus was to physically remove Himself from public view in order to pray. Leaving the crowds behind was absolutely necessary for Him to properly commune with His Father. Someone has said that "solitude is not being alone; solitude is being with God." If we experience loneliness in the place of prayer, that is simply a sign that our hearts have not yet found their abiding place in God. It must not discourage us if we feel discomfort, distraction, or even boredom when we first begin to seek our Bridegroom in the secret place. The first thing we learn, once we begin to embrace solitude, is just how addicted we are to everything *but* prayer.

Intimate prayer requires ever-increasing levels of privacy. We will never experience the quality of intimacy we desire with God until we learn to go beyond the veil and leave the distraction of human interaction behind. We often have the idea that God is far away, and prayer somehow brings Him near. That is not the problem, however. The problem is that God is too near! He is *so* near to us, in fact, that we have grown desensitized to His Presence. The omnipresent attribute of God means that He is *always everywhere at every moment.* We are never *where* He is *not.* When we walk into a room, we are not actively aware of the oxygen that is there. Although we would die without it, we are totally unaware of its presence. Involuntarily we breathe in and out without thinking. Each time we do, we are interacting with the air in the room. So it is with God. *Disengaging* ourselves from the noise and activity of life is the first step to *engaging* the reality of God's Presence.

Learning the Value of Lingering

Not only did Jesus often withdraw from the crowds to pray in solitude, but He also spent extended periods of time in prayer. You may struggle at first to spend even a few minutes in prayer, much less hours. As you begin to experience the affections of Christ, the time you spend in prayer will no doubt drastically increase. After our Church experienced a powerful outpouring of the Holy Spirit, our meetings often lasted late into the night as people wanted to bask in the Presence of God. As the evening grew long, people quietly slipped out until at last only a handful of us remained. It was not uncommon for a secondary outpouring of the Spirit of God to fall upon those who remained. We even found a name for this secondary experience of grace. We called it the "second wave." Learning to linger and wait *will* be rewarded. Setting time goals in prayer, however, is *not* a good idea in my opinion. Whether you spend three minutes or three hours a day in prayer will not change God's love for you. We love our children when they are toddlers just learning to walk. Their faltering steps are no less important than the confident strides that come with practice. Whether your prayer life is faltering or flourishing it is still cherished by God. Let your prayer life grow at its own pace. You will find that the more sensitive you become to the Presence of God, the more time you will *want* to spend in prayer.

Learning to Welcome the Holy Spirit

The ability to listen and hear God's voice requires the anointing of the Holy Spirit. In the *Song,* the Shulamite calls for the winds to come and enter her garden.

> Awake, O **north wind**, and come, O **south wind**! Blow upon my garden, let its fragrance be wafted abroad. Let my beloved come to his garden, and eat its choicest fruits.[243]

The Holy Spirit is the wind who awakens our hearts to the

---

[243] Song of Songs 4:16 RSV

Presence of God in prayer. In Hebrew, He is called the *Ruach Hakkodesh.* Ruach means "wind" or "breath." The imagery of the wind entering the Shulamite's garden is a picture of the Bride being filled with the Holy Spirit. The north wind presents a powerful, untamable wind. The south wind represents the gentle, comforting quality of the Holy Spirit. We can place no limitations upon the Spirit of God. We cannot have the comforting Presence of the Holy Spirit without also welcoming that part of Him that blows like a mighty wind, clearing away the debris of our hearts. In the final chapter of the book of Revelation, we read that the "Spirit and the Bride say, 'Come.'[244] The Bride does not resist nor quench nor grieve the Holy Spirit. She *cooperates* with His work in preparing her for her destiny.

Intimate Prayer and Spiritual Discernment

Intimate prayer is the portal into the supernatural realm of the Spirit of God. The Bible says that "the natural man cannot receive the things of the Spirit of God because they are spiritually discerned."[245] As our relationship with our Bridegroom deepens and becomes more intimate, we will find that our depth of revelation will also increase. The link between intimacy and increased revelation can be seen in the life of the Apostle John.

John is a type of the Bride. His name means "the beloved," and three times in his Gospel, John is called "the disciple whom Jesus loved," indicating a special depth of relationship. While the other apostles faced persecution and martyrdom (a picture of the Tribulation), John was safely exiled to the isle of Patmos (a picture of the Rapture). He was the only apostle who did not die as a martyr and serves to portray the Bride who will also be spared the martyrdom of the Tribulation period.

[244] Revelation 22:17
[245] 1 Corinthians 2:9-14

Secrets Revealed

During the final Passover meal, Jesus revealed that one of His followers would soon betray Him. The disciples began to question who it might be. Peter, knowing the special access that John had to Jesus, asked him to find out who the traitor was.

> One of His disciples, whom Jesus loved, was lying close to the breast of Jesus; so Simon Peter beckoned to him and said, "Tell us who it is of whom He speaks." So lying thus, close to the breast of Jesus, he said to Him, "Lord, who is it?" Jesus answered, "It is he to whom I shall give this morsel when I have dipped it." So when He had dipped the morsel, He gave it to Judas, the son of Simon Iscariot.[246] [emphasis added]

With all the speculation that abounds regarding the possible identity of the Antichrist, it would seem that only the Bride will be made privy to that special information at the end of the age. Notice that twice it is said of John that he was *lying close to the breast of Jesus.* Only those who are lying close to the heart of the Bridegroom at the end of the age will be able to rightly discern the events that are unfolding around them.

Learning to Awaken to His Presence

Our prayers can change everything - but they need not change or produce *anything.* We don't pray because we need something. We pray because we need ***Someone.*** Praying in the secret place becomes our way of entering into an intimate relationship with Christ. Over time, our prayer life becomes a

---

[246] John 13:23-26 RSV

place where we feel comfortably present with God. We need not always bring Him our words. Simply being present is enough. Lovers can linger in each other's arms for hours without ever speaking, and the deeper we go in prayer, the more superfluous words actually become. In the *Song*, the Shulamite talks about how the presence of her Beloved lies silently between her breasts all through the night like a sachet of myrrh.[247]

Once while I was speaking to a group of people, Jesus suddenly made Himself very present to me. I don't mean to say that I saw Him, but I heard Him clearly say these words to me: *"I am delighted in you!"* In that moment, I was flooded with a very real sense of how much He really loved me. It had nothing to do with the quality of my message or ministry. It had to do with *me!* The joy of knowing that somehow my life was giving pleasure to Him overwhelmed me. Then, as quickly as He had made Himself known, He concealed Himself again. I was left to scramble to find my place in my lesson notes. I have learned that there is a playfulness about Christ that only His winsome Bride is awakened to. Because she spends time lingering in His Presence and listening for His voice, her heart is easily awakened when He calls. In the fifth chapter of the *Song*, the Bride speaks:

> I slept, *but my heart was awake.* Hark! my beloved is knocking. "Open to me, my sister, my love, my dove, my perfect one; for my head is wet with dew, my locks with the drops of the night." I had put off my garment, how could I put it on? I had bathed my feet, how could I soil them? My beloved put his hand to the latch, and *my heart was thrilled within me.* I arose to open to my beloved, and my hands dripped with myrrh, my fingers with liquid myrrh, upon the handles of the bolt. I opened to my beloved, but my beloved had turned and gone. My soul

[247] Song of Songs 1:13

failed me when he spoke.[248] [emphasis added]

I have learned that Jesus is the "God of the Inopportune Moment." In the passage you just read from the *Song*, the Bridegroom arrived in the early hours of the morning while it was still dark. In the parable of the Ten Virgins we're told that the Bridegroom *delayed* his coming, and when he finally did arrive, it was at *midnight*. Jesus was even late to perform His first miracle! When He arrived at the wedding at Cana, the ceremony had already taken place, and the seven day wedding party was already in progress. Indeed, "the wind [Spirit] blows where it wills"[249] and even *when* it wills. As your relationship with your Bridegroom develops in prayer, you will find that He will not confine Himself to the prayer closet. He will call upon you at the most inopportune times and in the most inopportune places. This is described by the Bride in the *Song:*

> The voice of my beloved! Behold, he comes, leaping upon the mountains, bounding over the hills. My beloved is like a gazelle, or a young stag. Behold, there he stands behind our wall, gazing in at the windows, looking through the lattice..."[250] [emphasis added]

My wife, Rebecca, in teaching on these verses, has pointed out the deeper significance of the wall, the windows and the lattice. The walls represent the fears we develop in life. To protect our hearts from pain, we often build walls that keep people from getting too close. The Bridegroom, however, is not kept at bay by our walls of defense. He leaps over them with ease and takes His stand in our lives. Lattices are facades we strategically place in

---

[248] Song of Songs 5:2-6 RSV
[249] John 3:8
[250] Song of Songs 2:8 RSV

front of ourselves to hide the truth about who we are. We might grow beautiful flowers upon our "lattices," giving people the impression that all is right in our lives. But Jesus "looks through" all of our pretense. The Hebrew word for "windows" is the word *challown* (ןולח), and it means "to be pierced." It represents the painful wounds we receive in life. Once, while Rebecca was teaching this to a group of women at a retreat, one of the women told about a dream she had after hearing this message. In her dream, she saw herself crouching in a small, stone cubicle. It was completely dark inside, robbing her of her bearings. She could not tell which direction was up or down. Then suddenly, something pierced through the stone, and a single shaft of light streamed into the blackness. Then came another piercing thrust and another shaft of light entered the darkness. When she awoke from the dream, she realized the truth of what Rebecca had been sharing. *God will use the painful wounds that we receive in life as points of entry into the dark, hidden places of our souls.* Through those "windows" of emotional pain, His healing light enters in.

PART TWO

14

THE BEGINNING OF THE END

"We have taken the city of God. We are entering the Messianic era for the Jewish people, and I promise to the Christian world that what we are responsible for we will take care of."

Rabbi Shlomo Goren

The Capturing of the Temple Mount

On June 7, 1967, during the Six-Day War, Israeli Brigadier General Shlomo Goren led a group of fifty soldiers onto the site where the Second Temple of the Jews once stood. The faithful group fought their way past Muslim guards to reach the sacred spot. Once there, they conducted a jubilant prayer service at the very place where the next and final Jewish Temple will be built. Standing on what Jews feel is the literal center of the universe, Brig. Gen. Goren lifted a shofar to his lips and sounded an alarm. The haunting sound of the ancient ram's horn sent shock waves between heaven and earth and quite possibly signaled the beginning of the end!

The victory of the Six Day War and the reunification of Jerusalem took Jews around the world by utter surprise. Suddenly Jerusalem was under sovereign Jewish control for the first time in approximately two thousand years! Israel's chief rabbis had to quickly decide what course to take. On one hand, the capture of the Temple Mount meant it was now possible for the Jews to reinstitute Temple worship. On the other hand, to pursue that course would most certainly lead to world-wide condemnation of the Jewish state and a violent backlash.

Within a week after Goren's little band of faithful followers had declared the Temple Mount "liberated," the Chief Rabbinate of Israel ordered the holy site off-limits to Jews. The rabbis claimed that setting foot on the Temple Mount might possibly desecrate the spot where the Holiest of Holies once stood. It was a clever decision which appealed to the religious sensibilities of those Jews who were eagerly pushing for an immediate restoration of Temple worship. Their edict put everything indefinitely "on hold." There were many Jews, however, who believed the recapturing of Jerusalem and the Temple Mount was irrefutable evidence that the final days of the earth had begun. Today, many Jews in Israel hold to that belief and are doing everything they can to work toward the rebuilding of the Third Temple which they believe will prepare the way for the appearance of the Messiah. According to an ancient prophecy, their labors may not be in vain!

Daniel's Vision of a Ram and a Goat

About 2,500 years ago, the prophet Daniel was shown a vision that related to the Last Days. In the vision, he was transported about 150 miles north from Babylon to the Persian city of Susa. At that time, Babylon was the wonder of the world but in a little over a decade that would all change when Susa would become the capital city of the Medo-Persian Empire. The Spirit of God transported Daniel years into the future to behold a three-part vision that would have meaning for us today!

The Ram

In the first part of the vision, Daniel saw a ram standing in the east charging toward the north, south, and west. The ram was very powerful and had two horns - one longer than the other. An angel, who was sent to interpret the vision to Daniel, explained that the ram represented the Medo-Persian Empire that would arise after Babylon. The two horns on the ram's head represented the Medes and the Persians who jointly ruled the empire. The Persians were the stronger of the two and were represented by the longer of the two horns.

The Goat

In the second part of the vision, Daniel beheld a strong goat arising from the west to challenge the power of the ram. The goat possessed one powerful horn in the middle of its head. The angel told Daniel that the goat represented a King of Greece. Daniel watched as the goat attacked the ram and trampled it underfoot. However, shortly thereafter the goat's horn was broken off and four smaller horns took its place. History tells us that Alexander the Great marched westward from Greece and conquered the Medo-Persian Empire. His victories were short-lived, however, and upon his death his kingdom was divided between four of his generals just as Daniel had seen.

The Third Part of the Vision

In the third and last part of Daniel's vision, he saw yet another ruler emerging from what remained of one of the four kingdoms of Alexander's Empire. This ruler, who is yet to arise, will desire to dominate and ultimately destroy Israel. He will set himself up as their "prince" by helping in the re-building of their

Temple. But then he will betray them by bringing an end to the daily sacrifices and desecrating the Temple.[251] Daniel, of course, was envisioning the future Antichrist who will appear at the End of Days.

Eavesdropping on Angels

In the final part of Daniel's vision, he overheard a conversation between two angelic beings. One angel asked the other the following question:

> "How long will it take for the vision to be fulfilled—the vision concerning the daily sacrifice, the rebellion that causes desolation, and the surrender of the sanctuary and of the host that will be trampled underfoot?"

In other words, when will the Last Days (at which time these events will take place) begin to be fulfilled? The other angel told him that in 2,300 days the "sanctuary will be reconsecrated."

Doing the Math

In the Bible, days are often used as a representation of years or even 1,000 year periods. In this instance, I believe the 2,300 days represent years. The starting point from which to count 2,300 years is the time when Alexander's kingdom was divided into four parts. To be as accurate as possible, we know that Alexander was born 356BC. He died 323BC and his military campaigns lasted about ten years. So, it is most likely that his kingdom was divided sometimes between the years 333 and 323BC. If we use those dates as a reference point, and subtract

---

[251] This refers to the Third or final physical Temple of the Jews which has not yet been built.

them from 2,300 years we arrive at a ten year "window of time" between 1967 and 1977. Amazingly, June 7, 1967 (the date when the Temple Mount was recaptured by the Jews) falls perfectly within this narrow window of time! The words of God spoken through a prophet over 2,500 years ago are proven to be 100% accurate! *But there is something even more amazing about this story!*

The Title Deed

King David wanted to build a sanctuary where God could dwell on earth but it was his son, Solomon, who would have that honor. Nevertheless, David still had a part in building the Temple by providing the land where it would be built as well as amassing a fortune to finance its construction. The land where the Temple was eventually constructed originally belonged to a Jebusite (non-Jew) named, Araunah.[252] According to the biblical account, Araunah wanted to give the land to David, but David refused it as a gift saying, *"No, I insist on paying you for it. I will not sacrifice to the LORD my God burnt offerings that cost me nothing."* [253] If, David had not *paid* for the land, the claim of rightful ownership might be ambiguous today. But thanks to David's foresight, there can be no doubt that the land legally belongs to the Jews.

The Threshing Floor

The land that David bought from Araunah was a *threshing floor.* A threshing floor is a place where grain is brought during the harvest so that it can be separated from the outer husk or chaff. That threshing floor would later become the foundation of the Jewish Temple built by Solomon. The third and last Temple that has yet to be built – will be built on that same "threshing

[252] Some Bibles call him "Ornan." His name means "to be strong."
[253] 2 Samuel 24:24 NIV

floor" and will be a reconstitution of Solomon's Temple.

The Prophetic Significance of June 7, 1967

I've already shown how the recapturing of the Temple Mount in 1967 fits perfectly into Daniel's narrow prophetic window. But could that little-known event really mark the moment the Jewish Temple was reconsecrated and made ready to be rebuilt? You *will* believe once you consider the meaning of Shlomo Goren's name! His name in Hebrew means:

Shlomo = *Solomon*
Goren = *Threshing Floor*

Consider the remarkable nature of what happened! In fulfillment of a vision that had been given to Daniel thousands of years before, a man literally named "Solomon's Threshing-floor" stood on the actual site of King Solomon's original threshing floor, blew a ram's horn, and ushered in the era of the Last Days! Thus, the way has indeed been paved for the rebuilding of the future Jewish Temple and the final events of the history of mankind!

A Mysterious Man

On June 7, 1967, something else mysteriously occurred.[254] Salamon Gershon, one of the fifty soldiers who helped liberate the Temple Mount, recounts the following story of what happened that remarkable day. He said that as he and the other soldiers were walking on the Temple Mount, a man approached who spoke to them in English. He said that he had come to show them the exact location of the ruined Temple. He proceeded to show the

---

[254] See: www.templemountfaithful.org/s5760.htm

group the precise locations of such things as the Holy of Holies and the altar. According to Salamon, the man spoke with great excitement as he repeatedly blessed and thanked the group for their part in recapturing the Temple Mount. The mysterious man went on to say that he had been sent by God to tell them that the Arab occupation of Israel had ended forever! He made it clear to them that it was now time to rebuild the Third Temple in the same location he had shown them. According to Salamon's eyewitness account, when the mysterious man had finished speaking he vanished from their sight "as if he had been blown away by a wind." Salamon was so moved by the unusual encounter with the mysterious man, he went on to establish an organization dedicated to the rebuilding of the future Jewish Temple called the "Temple Mount and Land of Israel Faithful Movement"[255].

---

[255] See: www.templemountfaithful.org

15

THE LAST HARVEST

Be patient, therefore, brethren, until the coming of the Lord. Behold, the farmer waits for the precious fruit of the earth, being patient over it until it receives the early and the late rain.

Book of James

The Bible speaks not only of the events of the past, but also of the present and future. While a Bridal theme runs throughout the length of the Bible, the marriage of Jesus to His spiritual Bride is one of those prophetic events linked *specifically* to the end of time. Therefore, we should expect that before Jesus returns, His Bride will be literally present on the earth. I believe we are witnessing the beginning of that very thing! Not too long ago the general consensus was that the Church and the Bride were synonymous terms. In recent years, however, that has begun to change, and interest in the subject of the Bride of Christ is growing exponentially. In this chapter, I will present a paradigm for the events leading up to and surrounding the return of Jesus for His Bride.

The Seven Feasts of Israel

In the Old Testament, God appointed seven feasts to be observed during different seasons of the year. Three of the feasts occurred in the spring during the early harvest, one was celebrated in the summer, and the final three were observed in the fall during the final harvest. These seven feasts represent certain events that will ultimately be fulfilled by the Messiah. In fact, the first four feasts have *already* been fulfilled by Jesus Christ, while the final three still await their fulfillment. The final three feasts represent the final harvest cycle of souls before the end of days.

Passover

When Jesus was crucified, it was not on an arbitrary day. It happened on Passover because Jesus was and is both the *fulfillment* and the *fulfiller* of all the law and the prophets. He became the fulfillment of Passover by literally *becoming* the "lamb who [took] away the sins of the world."[256]

Unleavened Bread

The next feast, the Feast of Unleavened Bread, occurred the day after Passover. Leaven represents the presence of sin, thus *unleavened* bread represents the sinless Messiah.[257] During the Passover meal, called the Seder, a piece of unleavened bread called the *afikomen* is broken into two pieces. One piece is wrapped in a napkin and hid. At the conclusion of the meal, a child is sent to fetch the hidden bread. It is brought back to the table, and the entire family eats a portion of it. The word "afikomen" means "that which comes back later" and provides a beautiful picture of the resurrection of Christ. His body, like the afikomen, was broken, wrapped for burial, and hidden in a tomb. Later, He rose from the dead as the bread of heaven that feeds all who are spiritually hungry! Jesus was buried *precisely* on the Feast of Unleavened Bread, thus fulfilling the purpose of that feast.

---

[256] John 1:29

[257] John 6:35

First Fruits

The third feast, First Fruits, was celebrated on the third day. A bundled sheaf of barley was taken from the early harvest and waved before the Lord as an offering. The sheaf represented the first and best part of the total harvest that was to come. It was presented to God as a tithe. This was not a *single* stalk of barley but a *bundled* sheaf. When Jesus was crucified, the Bible tells us that the graves of some of the Old Testament saints opened. They were the first to experience the reality of the Resurrection!

> Jesus cried out again with a loud voice, and yielded up His spirit. Then, behold, the veil of the temple was torn in two from top to bottom; and the earth quaked, and the rocks were split, and the graves were opened; <u>and many bodies of the saints who had fallen asleep were raised; And coming out of the graves after His resurrection, they went into the holy city, and appeared to many</u>.[258] [emphasis added]

Were these saints of old "bundled" along with Jesus to become part of the firstfruit sheaf offering that was waved before God in Heaven? Personally, I think so! Consider what the Apostle Paul said:

> "But now Christ is risen from the dead, and has become the **firstfruits** of those who have fallen asleep."[259] [emphasis added]

As you can see, the first three feasts were all celebrated in succession. The fourth feast, called the Feast of Pentecost, was not

---

[258] Matthew 27:50-53
[259] 1 Corinthians 15:20

observed until fifty days later.

Pentecost

Again, it was precisely on the Feast of Pentecost that the Holy Spirit was given to the Church. This explains why the disciples were "all together in one place" at the time of the outpouring of the Spirit. It was not happenstance that caused them to gather on that exact day to wait for the promise of the Spirit. As Jews, they well understood that the feast days were God's way of marking time for the Jewish people.

> And when the day of Pentecost *had fully come*, they were all with one accord in one place.[260]

Two Prophetic Time Clocks

The seven feasts are indeed God's timepiece as times and seasons relate to His first covenant people, the Jews. When Jesus came in the flesh, He came exclusively to his brethren, the Jews.[261] He strictly forbade His disciples to preach the Kingdom of God to Gentiles. For three and a half years, He reached out to the Jews, only to be rejected by them. Finally, near the end of His earthly ministry, He wept over the rejection He had received at their hands and said:

> O Jerusalem, Jerusalem, the one who kills the prophets and stones those who are sent to her! How often I wanted to gather your children together, as a hen gathers her chicks under her wings, and you were not willing! See,

---

[260] Acts 2:1
[261] See Matthew 10:5 and 15:24

> your house is left to you desolate; For I say to you, you shall see me no more till you say, "Blessed is He who comes in the name of the Lord."[262] [emphasis added]

Thus, the ministry of Jesus to His brethren ended with their house left in ruins. But their chosen status will not always remain in ruins. In pronouncing their house desolate, He also included a redemptive promise. He said it would remain desolate - *until*. "Until" is a wonderful Biblical word that often translates as *hope!* It means that the ruins of the house of Israel will be rebuilt on a future day! It will be the day when they say to Jesus, "Blessed is He who comes in the name of the Lord."

Because of their initial rejection of Him, God turned His attention away from the Jews and placed it upon the rest of mankind. A new dispensation of time began as the Gospel began to spread beyond the confines of Jerusalem to the rest of the world. When the Gentiles began to hear and respond to the Gospel, God began to mark time prophetically according to His dealings with them. The Bible calls this way of marking time the "times of the Gentiles."[263]

When the dispensation of the Gentiles has run its course, God has promised to return and restore Israel to her former status. Their restoration, however, cannot take place until the age of the Gentiles comes to an end. Jesus said that Jerusalem would be under the control of the Gentile nations UNTIL the times of the Gentiles were fulfilled.[264] For two thousand years, that is exactly what happened. The Gentiles trod Jerusalem under foot as everyone sought to make it their capital city. Then, in June of 1967, the Israeli army breached the wall of the Old City and took back the political control of Jerusalem. As already stated, I believe

---

[262] Matthew 23:37-39

[263] Luke 21:24

[264] See Luke 21:24b

this was the beginning of the end of the "times of the Gentiles." It was not a *total* end of their control since the Jews quickly gave back custodial power of the Temple Mount to the Muslims. Nevertheless it was a "shot heard around the world," as it signaled the start of a major prophetic shift.

The Way of the Harvest

Well-respected prophetic voices have long been describing the coming of the "greatest revival the world has ever seen." Without a doubt, the Church *is* experiencing phenomenal growth in specific regions of the world. But should we really expect a great worldwide return to God at the end of the age? The Bible tends to say just the opposite. Personally, I am *for* revival whenever and wherever it happens. However, the notion of a great, end-time harvest does not seem to line up with the pattern of the final harvest which God has given us in His Word.

The Beginning of the Harvest

The Jews were commanded by God to harvest their fields in a prescribed manner. I believe the way they harvested their fields is a picture of how God is harvesting the "field of the world" and the souls of mankind.

The first part of the Jewish harvest was called "First Fruits." It constituted a tithe of the field. A priest would diligently search the fields until he found the grains that were ripening first. That portion of the field was then marked so as not to be disturbed. Plants that had come from outside of Israel were not included in this offering; neither any that came from the field of a non-Jew. The *first* ripening fruit was harvested at the very beginning of the harvest season and given to God as an offering.

As already stated, Jesus along with others who were raised from the dead at the time of His Crucifixion became the first fruits of God's harvest of the world.

The Great Harvest

After the first fruits had been gathered, the remainder of the field was gathered in what was called the "General Harvest" or the "Great Harvest." As workers moved through the field, the harvest naturally *dwindled* in size and scope with every pass that was made.

Gleanings

The last and final harvest of the field was called the "Gleanings." God commanded His people to leave a portion of their field as an offering for the poor.

> When you reap the harvest of your land, you shall not reap your field to its very border, neither shall you gather the **gleanings** after your harvest. And you shall not strip your vineyard bare, neither shall you gather the fallen grapes of your vineyard; <u>you shall leave them for the poor and for the sojourner</u>: I am the LORD your God.[265] [emphasis added]

Do you see the natural progression of the harvest? It does not *grow* in scope - *it diminishes.* I'm sure any farmer would welcome the mysterious appearance of an abundance of grain in his field at the end of harvest time. *But this is not the way of the harvest.* Some might argue that the great, end-time revival doesn't fit the pattern

---

[265] Leviticus 19:9-10 RSV

of the Jewish harvest cycle because it is *miraculous* in nature and overrides the normal way of doing things. Then why did God give us a *pattern* in His Word for the harvest if His plan was to ignore the pattern and do something totally different?

Who are the Poor?

I think we should at least consider the possibility that the final spiritual harvest of the earth will not be the greatest revival the world has ever seen, as many have predicted. Instead, it will be a narrowly specific revival given to a particular group of people identified as the "spiritually poor" of the earth. Who, then, are the poor of whom Jesus said, "theirs is the kingdom of God?"[266] The answer to this question is found in the letter of Paul to the church at Rome.

> Now if their [Israel's] fall is <u>riches</u> for the world, and their failure <u>riches for the Gentiles</u>, how much more their fullness! (lit. inclusion)[267] [emphasis added]

When Israel rejected Jesus as their Messiah, their house became desolate (ἔρημος lit. poor, abandoned, laid waste). It will remain so *until* their restoration at the end of the age.[268] At the time of their rejection, the Gentile nations received a transfer of the spiritual riches that belonged to Israel. It was a temporary transfer, however. Those who think God replaced Israel with the Church fail to see that a promise remains to restore Israel to her rightful riches and former glory. Indeed, *"the scepter shall **not** depart from Judah!"*[269] As the end of time approaches, the General

---

[266] Matthew 5:3
[267] Romans 11:12
[268] See Matthew 23:38
[269] Genesis 49:10

Harvest of the earth among the Gentile nations is coming to an appropriate end. According to the Apostle Paul, the spiritual poverty that was imposed upon Israel will end as well, at the point when "the fullness of the Gentiles [has] come in."[270] When the General Harvest ends, the field of the world will be opened to the poor (Israel). They will glean the final harvest of the ages during the final seven years of the history of the world. *It is a harvest that has been reserved just for them!*

> Blessed are the poor in spirit: for theirs is the kingdom of heaven.[271]

The "Sixth" Day War

The spiritual harvest cycle of the world began some two thousand years ago when Jesus was raised from the dead and offered up to the Father as a First Fruits wave offering. He was a literal *tithe* of the entire harvest, which still lay in the field of the world. Then, three and a half years later, at the home of a Gentile named Cornelius, the General Harvest of the Gentile world began and has continued ever since. Then, in 1967, the Jews regained political control of the holy city after almost two thousand years of enemy occupation. *The "times of the Gentiles" was fulfilled before our very eyes!* The manner in which God marked time changed once more. Already the harvest field is opening to those who have been spiritually poor. Now, God is once again marking time according to His people, Israel. All eyes should be upon Israel because everything that God will do from this point on relates primarily to the people and the land. Soon, the remaining three feasts of the Lord will be fulfilled. *Perhaps in our lifetime!*

---

[270] Romans 11:25
[271] Matthew 5:3

It's interesting that the war Israel fought in 1967 was miraculously won in the short space of *six days* and is remembered as the "Six Day War." Could it be that God was saying that the "sixth day" of human history had finally arrived and now the days of Israel's restoration had begun? *I think so!*

The Feast of Trumpets

Already the world grows dark and dangerous as the favor of the Lord is being lifted off the nations of the world and returned to Israel. For two thousand years, Jesus has been the light to the Gentiles. Now, in these last days, He is once more becoming the glory of Israel![272]

According to the Jewish calendar, the Feast of Trumpets, called *Yom Teruah* (העורת), marks the beginning of the "Latter Harvest." It begins on the first day of the Jewish month of Tishri and signals the beginning of the autumn of the year. Each year, we host a ministry school in Texas which begins on the day of the Feast of Trumpets.[273] It is logical to believe that just as Jesus Christ literally fulfilled the first four feasts of Israel, He will return to bring the final three feasts to completion. *The Feast of Trumpets is the next feast awaiting its prophetic fulfillment.*

A Day for Blowing Trumpets

Exactly what does the Feast of Trumpets pre-figure? The theme of this Feast, as its name implies, is the blowing of trumpets. The word "trumpet" actually refers to a ram's horn, called a *shofar.* Shofars were used by ancient Israel as a means of calling people to an event. They were used to call a general assembly and to rally men to battle. They were blown at the

---

[272] Luke 2:32

[273] For information about the Shulamite School, go to www.shulamiteministries.org.

coronation and anointing of kings, and they were blown at *weddings as well*! In ancient times, when the bridegroom came to abduct his bride for her wedding (see chapter 9), someone in the wedding party ran slightly ahead of the procession to announce their arrival. As he drew close to the bride's house, he would blow a shofar to signal the approach of the bridegroom's entourage. This was done to awaken the bride, should she be sleeping, so that she could join her bridegroom.

Jewish Figures of Speech

Every culture has its own figures of speech which include certain idioms and euphemisms that appear foreign to people outside of that culture. An example of this is the saying, "It is raining cats and dogs." The Bible also contains figures of speech common to the Jewish culture which are not readily familiar to those who are not Jewish. For example, when a certain man excused himself from following Jesus by saying, "Let me first go and bury my father,"[274] that was a figure of speech which really meant, "Let me take care of my father *until* he dies."

The Last Trump

Another figure of speech found in the Bible is the term "the last trump" which is used by Paul to describe the Rapture of the Bride:

> In a moment, in the twinkling of an eye, at the **last trumpet**. For the trumpet will sound, and the dead will be raised incorruptible, and we shall be changed.[275] [emphasis added]

[274] Luke 9:59
[275] I Corinthians 15:52

A common mistake is made when it is assumed that the "last trump" Paul writes about in these verses is synonymous with the last of the seven trumpets of God's wrath in John's vision of the Revelation.[276] In fact, the term "Last Trump" is actually a Jewish figure of speech which refers to the Feast of Trumpets.

Three Trumpets

Three of the Feasts of the Lord were called "trumps" by the Jews. Pentecost was called the "First Trump," The Feast of Trumpets was called the "Last Trump," and the Day of Atonement was called the "Great Trump." Even though the Feast of Trumpets falls *between* the First Trump and the Great Trump, it is still called the "Last Trump" because it was the last warning from God that the Day of Atonement (Judgment) was fast approaching. By understanding the Jewish roots of the Scriptures, it becomes clear that the timing of the Lord's return for His Bride will occur on some future Feast of Trumpets!

The Open Door of Heaven

In the fourth chapter of the book of Revelation, there is a depiction of the Bride's sudden abduction. The Apostle John, who serves as a type of the Bride of Christ,[277] heard the voice of Jesus sounding like a *trumpet.*

> After this I looked, and, behold, **a door was opened in Heaven:** and the first voice which I heard was as it were of a **trumpet** talking with me; which said, **Come up hither,**

---

[276] Revelation 11:15

[277] That John is a representation of the Bride can be seen in the fact that (a) his name means "the Beloved", (b) he was the only Apostle who was spared a martyr's death, and (c) he was Jesus' closest companion, called the "disciple that Jesus loved."

> and I will shew thee things which must be hereafter.[278] [emphasis added]

The sound of the trumpet was synonymous with the door of Heaven opening and John ascending upward.

It's interesting that, in the Bible, God commanded the eastern gate of the Temple to be opened at two specific times: on the Sabbath and on the Feast of Trumpets (the new moon)!

> Thus says the Lord GOD: The gate of the inner court that faces east shall be shut on the six working days; but on the Sabbath day it shall be opened and on the day of the new moon it shall be opened.[279][emphasis added]

Since Messiah will enter Jerusalem through the eastern gate at the end of time, the opening of the east gate is a beautiful picture that points us to the exact timing of the Bridegroom's return on some future Feast of Trumpets!

Wiggle Room

I am not saying that I *definitively* know the exact moment that Jesus will return, and that is because a certain amount of ambiguity exists as it relates to the Feast of Trumpets. It is the ***only*** Feast that cannot begin *until* the new moon has been seen and confirmed. This creates a possible delay, or "wiggle room," as it relates to the exact timing of the return of the Lord.

The Moon: A Symbol for the Bride

Why is the Feast of Trumpets linked to the appearing of a

[278] Revelation 4:1 KJV
[279] Ezekiel 46:1 KJV

new moon? The moon serves as a biblical symbol of God's people. In the book of Genesis, God gave the moon the authority to rule the darkness,[280] and Jesus gave His disciples authority to rule over the *powers* of darkness. As a celestial mirror, the moon produces no light of its own but simply reflects the light that emanates from the sun. As the Bride, our glory is the reflection of God's own glory. In the *Song*, the Bride is clearly described as the moon whose light is as "clear as the sun." She is a perfect reflection of her heavenly companion!

> Who is she who looks forth as the morning, Fair as the **moon**, clear as the sun, awesome as an army with banners?[281][emphasis added]

The New Moon

The appearance of the new moon signals the beginning of the Feast of Trumpets. Because it's called a "new" moon, it is logical to think that it refers to a *full* moon. In fact, just the opposite is true. A new moon occurs when the earth, sun and moon all align in such a way as to make the moon seem to disappear. It becomes *invisible* to the earth but fully *visible* to the sun. This heavenly configuration is sometimes referred to as the "marriage of the moon to the sun" and is a beautiful picture of the Bride vanishing from the earth at the moment of her Rapture to join her Bridegroom in heaven.

No Man Knows the Day or Hour

Another Jewish figure of speech is found in the statement Jesus made about "no man knowing the day or hour of His

---

[280] Genesis 1:16

[281] Song of Songs 6:10

return." In the Bible, the Feast of Trumpets is to begin on the first day of the Jewish month of Tishri. Until the new moon was verified, however, the shofars could not be blown nor could the Feast begin. In ancient times, the leader of the Jewish Sanhedrin assigned two priests the task of sighting the new moon. Beginning on the first day of Tishri, they would walk outside of the city each night, look up into the night sky, and observe the face of the moon. Without the benefit of modern telescopes, it was difficult to observe the disappearance of the last sliver of the moon's light. If the sky should be overcast, this would also preclude their task. Until both priests could agree that the new moon had occurred, the Feast could not begin. Therefore, although the Feast of Trumpets fell on the first day of Tishri, it might be two, three or more days before the shofar could be blown to signal the actual start of the Feast.[282]

As you can see, the need to verify the appearance of the new moon added an element of uncertainty to the Feast of Trumpets. Because of this unique ambiguity, the Jews referred to the Feast of Trumpets as "The Day Which No Man Knows!" When Jesus told His disciples that "no man could know the day or hour of His return,"[283] He was actually identifying the *very day* of His return! He was telling them, by use of a well known idiom, something they knew well from the oral teachings of their youth. Even today the Feast of Trumpets is called "The Hidden Day" and "The Day That No Man Knows" by Jews!

A Hidden Message?

Just as the Feast of Trumpets is known as "The Hidden Day" there seems to be a *hidden message* in the first verse of the

---

[282] Today, by tradition, the Feast of Trumpets is celebrated on the 1st and 2nd of Tishri as one long day.

[283] Matthew 24:36

book of Genesis. Jewish scholars believe that the world was created on the 1st day of Tishri (Feast of Trumpets) and it will end on the 1st of Tishri as well. The vast majority of rabbis hold to the view that the Earth was created around 6,000 years ago. This historical chronology is found in what is called the Jewish *Sedar Olam*[284] which is based on a literal interpretation of the book of Genesis. The words "in the beginning," seem to reveal a hidden message. When read backwards in the original Hebrew language, they spell out the phrase "the first of Tishri!"

While we still cannot know exactly *which* Feast of Trumpets will be the one marked for our Bridegroom's return, each year as the Feast approaches, we can look for its arrival with expectancy as we make ourselves ready for the possibility.

A Day Known Only to the Father

Another allusion to the timing of the Bride's Rapture is found in the words of Jesus concerning the fact that "only His Father knows the exact moment of His return."

> But of that day and hour no one knows, not even the angels of heaven, **but My Father only**.[285][emphasis added]

You will recall from our brief study of the Jewish wedding customs, that it was the bridegroom's father who determined *when* the wedding would take place.[286] The son had to wait for his father's permission to go and bring his bride to her wedding. In the ruling body of the Jewish Sanhedrin, there were two leaders. One held the office of the high priest and the other was called the ***Av Beit Din*** which means "the father of the house." When the two

---

[284] Two rabbinical works which provide a religious chronology of time and history.

[285] Matthew 24:36

[286] See chapter 6, The Abduction of the Bride

priests finally confirmed the sighting of the new moon, they reported their finding to the Av Beit Din (the father). Only ***he*** knew when he would give the order for the shofars to be blown. Thus, just as Jesus said - only the *Father* knows the exact time the shofar will sound!

The Great Debate

The debate rages on as to whether the Church will be taken out of the world before the days of Tribulation begin or whether she will go through part or all of the Tribulation. There are some very learned students of the Word who believe sincerely that the Church will go through the testing of the Tribulation period. On the other hand, there are others, like myself, who are convinced that the Rapture must happen before the beginning of the Tribulation period. *Who is right?* I have come to the conclusion that *both are right*. The Bride will be taken out of the world before the Great Tribulation and the Church will remain to endure that time.

Friends of the Bridegroom

There is a powerful prayer movement arising today being spear-headed by such leaders as Mike Bickle with the International House of Prayer.[287] It is a movement that is calling and preparing a company of people to live in radical relationship to Christ and their culture. Those who have been drawn to the message of this movement have embraced a theology that prepares them to steadfastly endure the trial of the Tribulation period. At the same time, there are others who are answering a

---

[287] See www.fotb.com

different call to *Become The Beloved.* They are not preparing themselves for great Tribulation; they are preparing themselves *for their Bridegroom*. Two very different callings. *Both are correct!*

Reconciling These Two Views

These two polar opposite views are irreconcilable unless we accept the precept that the Church and the Bride are *not* identifiably the same. The Bride is a separate remnant (rib) of people who are taken out of the greater *body* of Christ. While the idea that some will escape the Tribulation while others will be called to endure it may assault our fundamental sense of fairness, we must concede that God's ways are ultimately just and right, and He has a purpose for everything He does.

16

THE BRIDE MADE READY

Let us be glad and rejoice, and give honor to Him:
for the marriage of the Lamb is come
and His wife hath made herself ready.
The Book of Revelation

I have observed that many Christians today have adopted an attitude of indifference toward the subject of the coming of the Lord. I think this is because, in our present culture, the main concern of the average church member is how they might live well and be happy. There is little thought given to preparing for something that may or may not happen in their lifetime. Add to this the fact that most of us have been taught that it is impossible to "know the day or hour" of our Lord's return, and preparing for that day seems an exercise in futility. In contrast to this, the heart of the Bride longs for and prepares for the coming of her Bridegroom God.

Brides Have a Plan

Little boys rarely think about their future wedding days. I can assure you, however, that little girls do! They begin to plan for their wedding well in advance. When I am counseling for marriage, I advise couples to allow themselves a full year to plan their wedding. From experience, I know how stressful the preparations can become, especially in the last few weeks before the ceremony. As the special day approaches, I have seen how brides often become intensely laser-focused. Likewise, I think the Bride of Christ is sometimes misunderstood because of her high level of intensity and what seems like tunnel vision. While others can give their attention to many tasks, the Bride feels constrained to focus on one thing - *preparing herself for her Bridegroom.*

Three Brides

The love stories of Ruth, Esther and the Shulamite, give us a glimpse into how the Bride "makes herself ready."

Ruth

Ruth is instructed by her mother-in-law to go into the tent of Boaz and lie down at his feet in hopes that he might acknowledge her and agree to become her "kinsman redeemer."[288] Before doing so, however, Naomi tells her to first *prepare* herself by washing, anointing and clothing herself with a wedding garment.

> Wash yourself therefore and anoint yourself. Put on your best garment and go down to the threshing floor; but do not make yourself known to the man...[289]

I propose that washing herself with water is symbolic of the need to cleanse the outward dimension of our lives. You will recall that part of the ancient betrothal custom, called the *mikvah,* was done to separate the bride *unto* her husband. It was a promise to live

---

[288] According to Jewish law, a widow who had no son could request the next of kin marry her for her well-being as well as to continue the family bloodline.
[289] Ruth 3:3

circumspectly and remain a virgin until her wedding day. Those who answer the call to *Become The Beloved* understand that they too have been called to live according to a high standard of moral purity. The line between our spirituality and our sexuality is a thin one indeed. In fact, the two are inseparable since both spring from the same source - *our passion.* Our *sexual passion* is driven by our desire to *be desired* by another human being. Our *spiritual passion* is driven by our desire to be desired by *God.* I have often heard people praying for God to give them passion. There is no need to pray for passion. God has already given us all the passion we need. What we need to pray is that God would give us the strength and wisdom to *channel* our passion rightly. Knowing how to be in possession and control of our own sexuality is one of the most difficult things a person can do in a world lost and adrift in sexual confusion. But when we come to see how much our sexuality is actually an integral part of our spirituality, we *will* choose moral purity.

Ruth also anointed herself with oil. Oil symbolizes a deeper level of consecration. It speaks of the inner realm of our thoughts, intents and motives. Oil permeates the flesh of man. In our church, we once had a jar of oil which we used for anointing the sick. The jar was a light color green at first but slowly darkened as the oil actually permeated the porous composition of the jar. Over time, the oil and the jar became one. So it is with us when we welcome the Presence of the Holy Spirit to dwell with us and in us.

Finally, Naomi instructed Ruth to put on a special kind of raiment. The Hebrew word translated "raiment" is the word *simlah* (הלמש), and it refers to a thin garment which assumed the shape of the woman's body. We might liken it to lingerie, which is made to conform to and reveal the feminine shape. The Bride of Christ does not seek to hide her true "shape" or imperfections. She presents herself to Jesus with an honest heart and a willingness to be transparent and vulnerable to His gaze and assessment.

It is not a minor point to note that in the book of Revelation, as in the book of Ruth, the Bride makes *herself* ready. She does not wait for others to prepare her. She takes responsibility for her own spiritual condition before God.

Esther

Queen Esther also went through a season of preparation before she was given in marriage to the Persian King, Ahasuerus. Once again, we find the image of the bridal *mikvah* as Esther is bathed in the oil of myrrh for six months followed by six months of soaking in what the Bible calls "sweet odours," or balsam. The *Song of Songs* identifies myrrh as being the fragrance of the Bridegroom.[290] *Myrrh* (σμύρνα) means "suffering and death." It is produced by slicing the bark of the tree so that the blood- colored resin seeps out. As the resin emerges, it hardens into droplets called "tears." The calling of the Bride is to be identified with the sufferings of the Cross. She understands that living in the power of the Holy Spirit is much more than having a *powerful ministry*. She comprehends that true spirituality has more to do with *character* before God than *giftedness* before men. Those who are the Bride prepare themselves by "putting to death" the motivations of the flesh[291] and by allowing the Holy Spirit to strip away the thin veneer of the heart so that a true relationship with God might come forth.

I believe deeply in every believer's need to be personally baptized in the power and Presence of the Holy Spirit. I believe that we should earnestly seek to be endowed with spiritual gifts, and I highly value the anointing of the Holy Spirit. As I write this,

---

[290] Song of Songs 1:13-14
[291] Romans 8:13

however, I do so in the shadow of yet another painful and public demise of a Christian leader of national prominence. Without addressing his specific situation directly, I think it's important that we begin to address our unhealthy addiction to such leaders and turn our hearts instead to the deeper need we all have to immerse ourselves in an authentic relationship with Christ.

After soaking in myrrh for six months, Esther soaked in the oil of balsam for an additional six months. In ancient times, balsam was cultivated in the lush oasis of En-Gedi, located west of the Dead Sea. It is said that Mark Antony gave Cleopatra orchards in En-Gedi as gifts to win her love. In the *Song*, as in the book of Esther, both myrrh and balsam are mentioned as substances used in the preparation of the bride.

> A bundle of myrrh is my beloved unto me, That lies all night between my breasts. My beloved is to me as a cluster of henna blooms (balsam) In the vineyards of Engedi.[292] [emphasis added]

Henna, or balsam, was used as a healing agent in ancient times and symbolizes our need to be made whole from our human brokenness.

At our church in Texas, we encourage people to spend an extended time "soaking" their hearts in the Presence of the Lord. Like Esther's ritual bathing, we have learned that "soaking" has a purpose in the preparation process for us too.

The Song of Songs

In the *Song*, we find a third illustration of how the Bride is prepared for her wedding day. The entire book tells the

---

[292] Song of Songs 1:13-14

progressive story of how Abishag, as an insecure farm girl, is transformed both inwardly and outwardly by the persistent love and encouragement of her king. She too knows the value of time spent lingering in the arms of her Beloved. She refers to herself as being "lovesick" and describes how she faints into her lover's arms.

> He brought me to the banqueting house, and his banner over me was love. Stay me with flagons [wine], comfort me with apples: for I am sick of love. His left hand is under my head, and his right hand doth embrace me.[293]

Like Mary of Bethany, who was criticized for wasting her costly offering, there will always be those who accuse the *Beloved* of not working enough, serving enough, or being involved enough. Nevertheless, the heart that is set aflame by the sacred kiss of the Bridegroom is ruined for lesser pursuits, no matter how noble they might be.

The Days of Preparation

The Apostle Paul wrote to Timothy that a special reward, called the "crown of righteousness," awaits those who "love the appearing of the Lord."[294] Sadly, many believers today neither love nor do they even look forward to the day of the Lord's appearing. Sermons on the topic of His return are seldom heard anymore even though it's a cardinal doctrine of the Christian Church! Uninspired believers have drifted into either skepticism or apathy even though the Scriptures repeatedly urge us to discern the signs of the times. The return of Christ is called the

---

[293] Song of Songs 2:4-6 KJV
[294] 2 Timothy 4:8

"blessed hope,"[295] but many seem to hope it never happens - at least in *their* lifetime! Yet Jesus taught that those who love Him in every generation should watch and prepare for His return! The parable of the wise and foolish virgins alone teaches us of the supreme importance of being ready for the Bridegroom's sudden return.

The Months of Preparation

The days of the Bride's preparation are presented in the last three months of the Jewish calendar. The months of Av, Elul and Tishri are even called the "months of preparation" because they lead into the final three fall feasts of the Lord, which are:

- Feast of Trumpets (Yom Teruah)
- Day of Atonement (Yom Kippur)
- Feast of Tabernacles (Succoth)

The Jewish calendar is based on the moon, which cycles roughly every 29.5 days rather than 30 and 31 days. This causes an overlap in the way the Jewish months correspond with the months of our calendar. The Jewish month of Av, for example, usually falls between the months of July and August. The month of Elul occurs between the months of August and September, and the month of Tishri falls between the months of September and October.

The Fulfillment of the Last Three Feasts

Since Jesus has literally fulfilled the first four feasts, we should fully expect Him to fulfill the remaining three feasts as well. He will fulfill the Feast of Trumpets by returning for His

---

[295] Titus 2:13

Bride (the Rapture). He will fulfill the Day of Atonement when He appears seven years and ten days later as the Judge of all the earth. The Feast of Tabernacles will be fulfilled by Christ over a period of a thousand years when He rules and reigns from Jerusalem in what is called the Millennial Reign of Messiah on earth.

The Worst of Times

The book, *A Tale of Two Cities,* by Charles Dickens begins with the words "It was the best of times and it was the worst of times." The Jews consider the month of Av to be just that - the best and the worst time of the year. It is considered the "worst" time of the year because of one particular day: *the 9th of Av.* The 9th of Av is considered the most unfortunate day of the year for Jews and is observed with fasting, mourning and praying for protection from their enemies. The Jews believe it is the one day of the year in which the hatred of their enemies reaches a zenith and manifests in trouble for the Jews. Indeed, history affirms that the 9th of Av has often spelled disaster for the Jews. Most notably, it is the exact day on which both the Temple of Solomon and the second Temple built by Herod were destroyed 700 years apart! More recently, it was on the 9th of Av, 2005 that the Jewish government used its own military to forcibly remove Jewish settlers from the Gaza Strip, knowing that God has promised to judge those who dare divide His land![296]

I believe the month of Av represents the perilous times that will arise at the end of the age. Satan's hatred for the Jewish people will reach its zenith as he plots to bring all the nations of the world against them in an unholy alliance.

---

[296] Joel 3:2

The Best of Times

One of the most comforting phrases appearing repeatedly in the Bible is the phrase *"And it came to pass!"* And so it is with the 9th of Av. Once the *worst day* of the Jewish year has come and gone, the *best of times* is just around the corner! In the same way the 9th of Av is considered the worst day of the year for Jews, the 15th of Av is considered the very *best day* because it marks the days leading up to the Fall Feasts of the Lord. In a sense, the 15th of Av is like a pivotal hinge between the time of mourning and the time of gladness.

The Month of Av and the Dance of the Maidens

The latter part of the month of Av represents the time when the Bride of Christ will answer the call to arise in the earth. In ancient times, the 15th of Av was celebrated as a day when brides were chosen. According to the Talmud,[297] young women would purify white garments in a bridal mikvah[298] and wear them during a rite called the "Dance of the Maidens." The entire village gathered in a meadow or vineyard to watch the dance of celebration. Young men used this as an opportunity to spy out potential mates. As the maidens danced, they sang a traditional song of three verses. The first verse said, "Marry me for beauty, for a woman is made to be beautiful." The second verse was, "Marry me for children, for a woman is made to give children." The final verse said, "Marry me not for beauty or for children, but marry me so that you can adorn me with your own adornments." Sin-fallen man may think that by applying enough cosmetics to his soul (marry me for beauty) or by the effort of good works (marry me for children), he can make himself presentable to God. But the

[297] Talmud, Taanit 26b
[298] Ceremonial baptism

Bride does not promote her own virtues to her Bridegroom. She offers *herself* as a blank canvas upon which her Bridegroom might paint His own masterpiece. As the Bride of Christ, we begin our "days of preparation" by reflecting on the poverty of our own humanity in contrast to the surpassing riches of the grace and glory given freely to us by our Bridegroom. In the book of Revelation, we read:

> Then I, John, saw the holy city, New Jerusalem, coming down out of Heaven from God, prepared as a bride ***adorned*** for her husband.[299][emphasis added]

And in the book of Ephesians:

> Husbands, love your wives, just as Christ also loved the church, and gave Himself for her, that He might sanctify and cleanse her with the washing of water by the word, that He might present her to Himself a glorious church, not having spot, or wrinkle, or any such thing; but that she should be holy and without blemish.[300]

Christ is the One who adorns us, prepares us, sanctifies, and cleanses us! He alone makes us worthy of our high calling.

The Month of Elul

The month that follows Av is the month of ***Elul,*** and it represents the season of the beginning of the Bride's preparation. In fact, Elul is actually called the "month of preparation." It leads up to the Feast of Trumpets and the Day of Atonement, which mark the end of the seven-year feast calendar. Prophetically, this

---

[299] Revelation 21:2
[300] Ephesians 5:25-27

represents the end of time. The Day of Atonement is the final day of reckoning, when all accounts between God and man must be settled. Because of the awesomeness of the Day of Atonement, the Jews look upon the month of Elul as their time to "make themselves ready" to meet God and seek mercy for their sins.

In the *Song of Songs* and in I Kings, we are told that the bride of Solomon came from the region of Israel called Shunem - a territory of land allotted to the Tribe of Issachar. The Tribe of Issachar was known to be those who ***"had understanding of the times, to know what Israel ought to do."***[301] As the end of time grows nearer, those who comprise the Bridal Company will become more insightful of world events and more attuned to the leading of the Holy Spirit. While others grow complacent, apathetic, and even scoff at the idea of the nearness of the Bridegroom's return, the Bride will have confident prophetic insight into understanding the signs of the times. While others will go about their lives as usual, the Bride will be busy making herself ready for her wedding day and warning others to do the same.

The Meaning of Elul

The word "elul" means "to seek," and so the Bride prepares herself by devoting her heart to *seeking* the One she loves. Jewish tradition teaches that there is no other season when God makes Himself more accessible to man than during the 40-day period beginning with the start of Elul and ending on the Day of Atonement. The ancient Jews referred to this period as the days when *"The King was in the Field."* This is based on the idea that, when a king was enthroned in his palace, he was not easily accessible. An audience with him would be granted only to those who had merited his attention. Once a year, however, the king

[301] 1 Chronicles 12:32

would leave his palace to inspect his fields. When "the king was in the field" anyone could approach him. In the days just preceding the coming of the Lord, God will make Himself abundantly accessible to those who are willing to take the time to seek Him. That is the meaning of the verse found in Isaiah 55:6:

> Seek ye the LORD *while* He may be found, call ye upon Him *while* he is near. (KJV)

I believe we are living in the time when *the King is in the field.* God is calling His Bride into the secret place of intimate prayer. Those who seek Him will find Him.

Isaac and Rebecca

The Bible tells us that Isaac took a tent out to the field at the end of the day. He was there because he knew that his bride, Rebecca, would soon be appearing upon the horizon. I believe this is yet another prophetic picture of the Heavenly Bridegroom and His Bride at the end of the age. From parables Jesus taught, we know that the field represents the world. The fact that it was at the "end of the day" when Isaac pitched his tent is symbolic of the end of the age. The story goes on to say that Isaac began to "meditate" while in the field. The word for "meditate" is an intriguing Hebrew word. It is the word *suwach* (שוח). The meaning of the word is uncertain. Some scholars believe it means to "pray while walking about." Others feel it means simply to "muse or ponder in prayer." What makes this word *most* interesting is that it is used this one time only in the whole of the Bible. I believe *suwach* represents a kind of prayer that will be prayed once - *at the end of the age*. It is a picture of King Jesus, standing in the final harvest field of the earth, calling His Bride to come forth while making Himself accessible one last time for all those who will come. These are the days in which all mankind should seek the Lord while He may be found!

The Month of Tishri

When the "days of preparation" of Elul are complete, the first day of the month of Tishri arrives. This marks the beginning of the Feast of Trumpets. As already shown, Jesus will return on some future Feast of Trumpets to abduct His Bride. In ancient Israel, while the feast was heralded by the blowing of shofars, the priests in the Temple recited Psalm 24:

> Who may ascend into the hill of the LORD? Or who may stand in His holy place? He who has clean hands and a pure heart, Who has not lifted up his soul to an idol, nor sworn deceitfully. He shall receive blessing from the LORD, And righteousness [lit. vindication] from the God of his salvation.[302]

While this may speak of Christ's ascension into heaven after His resurrection, could it not also be asking who will ascend in the Rapture on the Feast of Trumpets? *Those who have made themselves ready!*

Holy Convocations

In the Old Testament, God established meeting times with His people called "holy convocations."[303] Each Sabbath is a holy convocation, as are the seven Feasts of Jehovah.

These are the feasts of The Lord, *holy convocations,* which

---

[302] Psalm 24:3-5

[303] Hebrew *mik-raw*, "a called assembly".

you shall proclaim at their appointed times.[304]

The first disciples were Jewish and lived according to the cycle of the holy convocations. This is why they gathered together "when the Day of Pentecost was fully come."[305] Pentecost was a holy convocation! Four of the holy convocations have been literally fulfilled by Jesus. Today, when the month of September[306] approaches, it signals the possible return of Jesus for His Bride! Thus, it is the season of the year when we should prepare for the very real possibility that our Bridegroom will return! No one can live in a state of imminent expectancy twenty four hours a day and seven days a week. Neither does God expect His *Beloved* to live this way. Sometimes people hear the message of the coming of the Lord and they feel that life has become meaningless in light of it. Why make plans? Why marry or bring children into a world destined to end? We are not to stop living just because we see the signs of the times advancing around us. We should live our lives to the fullest. We should live them, however, *in the light of eternity.*

---

[304] Leviticus 23:4

[305] Acts 2:1

[306] September and October correspond to the Jewish month of Tishri

17

THE WILD OLIVE TREE

So the children of Joseph, Manasseh and Ephraim,
took their inheritance.
Joshua 16:4

Replacement Theology

It is my opinion that the events of the Last Days can never be rightly understood without understanding God's plan for the Jews and how Gentiles fit into that plan. The people and land of Israel play a major role in the unfolding events of the End Times. But according to some, this is not the case. One of the greatest errors the Church has made is in the development of what is called "Replacement Theology." Perhaps you have never heard that term before, but the chances are you have been exposed to it in subtle forms. Every time you have heard someone refer to the Church as "spiritual Israel," you have entertained the notion of Replacement Theology. Every time you have heard someone teach that the Church is the restoration of the Tabernacle of David, you have heard a form of Replacement Theology. Often, sincere, well-meaning teachers pass along bits and pieces of Replacement Theology without even knowing it. In essence, Replacement Theology teaches that the Jews, as a people and nation, have been rejected by God because of *their* rejection of Jesus[307] as their Messiah. Therefore, they no longer hold a chosen status position

[307] "Yeshua" in Hebrew.

before God and have become just like any other people. In light of this, the term "Israel" becomes meaningless as it refers to the promises and plans of God; all of which have now been transferred to the Church. In a nutshell, the Church has essentially replaced Israel according to Replacement theologians. Various forms of this kind of thinking have unfortunately taken root in modern Christian thought.

The seeds of Replacement Theology can be traced all the way back to the first century Church at Rome. When Gentiles began to be saved and added to the church, disputes arose between the Jewish believers and their non-Jewish brothers. In AD 49, the Emperor Claudius expelled all Jews from Rome, which left the church comprised only of Gentile converts. It was during this time that the idea that God had set aside the Jews as His chosen people began to take form. Five years later, after the death of Claudius, the Emperor Nero welcomed the Jews back to the city. When they returned, they found the church reluctant to accept them back. Paul's letter to the Romans was written in an attempt to help restore his Jewish brothers to the fellowship of the church. His letter seeks to correct the false notion that God had rejected them. He makes this point quite clear in the 11th chapter of the book of Romans:

> I ask, then, has God rejected his people [Israelites]? By no means! I myself am an Israelite, a descendant of Abraham, a member of the tribe of Benjamin.[2] God has not rejected His people whom He foreknew.[308]

While it is true that in the present dispensation of time God has been focusing His attention primarily on the Gentile Church, He has by no means forsaken nor has He forgotten His eternal promises to Israel. The "gifts and the call of God are

---

[308] Romans 11:1-2 RSV

irrevocable."[309] He *will* return and restore her, not only to the physical land of her inheritance; but to Himself as well!

Clearly, most of Israel failed to recognize their "day of visitation" when Jesus came as their Messiah.[310] Just like Joseph before Him, "[Jesus] knew His brethren, but *they* knew [Him] not"[311] even though he stood before them in the flesh. Because of their unbelief, the house of Israel was reduced to an impoverished state.

> O Jerusalem, Jerusalem, killing the prophets and stoning those who are sent to you! How often would I have gathered your children together as a hen gathers her brood under her wings, and you would not! Behold, your house is forsaken. And I tell you, you will not see me ***until*** you say, 'Blessed is He who comes in the name of the Lord!'" [312][emphasis added]

The word "forsaken" ("desolate," KJV) is the Greek word *erēmos (ἔρημος)* and refers to a flock of sheep abandoned by their shepherd and left to care for themselves in the wild. This wasn't the first time the Jews were left to roam the wilderness. Thousands of years earlier, they wandered in the wilderness for forty years. But then as now, God did not utterly forsake or forget them! In fact, a faithful remnant was preserved to enter and take possession of the Promised Land. Although the majority of Jews today reject Jesus as their Messiah, we can rest assured that a faithful remnant *has* been preserved.

---

[309] Romans 11:29 RSV
[310] Luke 19:44
[311] Genesis 42:8 KJV
[312] Luke 13:34-35 RSV

The Important Word "Until"

The Apostle Paul made it clear that Israel's failure to accept Jesus as Messiah was partial and temporary.

> I want you to understand this mystery, brethren: a hardening has come upon **part** of Israel, **until** the full number of the Gentiles come in.[313] [emphasis added]

"Until" is a word of hope for Israel! Two thousand years ago, the spiritual riches of the house of Israel were transferred to the Gentile Church. But that is by no means the end of the story!

> Now if their trespass means riches for the world, and if their failure means riches for the Gentiles, how much more will their <u>full inclusion</u> mean![314][emphasis added]

Jesus said the house of Israel would remain desolate UNTIL a future day when they will acknowledge Him as their Messiah. Then they will say, "Blessed is He who comes in the name of the Lord!"[315]

Jesus also said Jerusalem would be under the control of the Gentile nations UNTIL the "times of the Gentiles [was] fulfilled."[316] That occurred on June 7, 1967 when the Jews reclaimed control of the city of Jerusalem and the words of Jesus were fulfilled in a war that lasted only six days![317] As the "times of the Gentiles" are even now drawing to a complete end, God's attention is turning back to Israel. The spiritual riches of God's

---

[313] Romans 11:25 RSV

[314] Romans 11:12 RSV

[315] Luke 13:34-35 RSV

[316] Luke 21:24

[317] The words of Jesus were only partially fulfilled, since the Gentiles will once again take control of Jerusalem during the final 3 ½ years of the Tribulation. See Revelation 11:2.

love and favor will soon be taken from the world and given back to her! As Gentiles, we have adopted the idea that the grace to be saved will always be available to us. However, the Bible clearly states that at some future date, the "times of the Gentiles" will end. The door will close. Then, as the world plunges into deep, spiritual darkness, Israel will experience a glorious spiritual re-awakening on a national scale!

> ...I want you to understand this mystery, brethren: a hardening has come upon part of Israel, until the full number of the Gentiles come in, and so all Israel will be saved; as it is written, "The Deliverer will come from Zion, he will banish ungodliness from Jacob" and this will be my covenant with them when I take away their sins.[318] [emphasis added]

The Party of the Second Part

In the Bible, God always built relationships with people by forging covenants with them. Israel was brought into relationship with God when she received His covenant mediated by Moses at Mt. Sinai. Replacement Theology is based on the idea that the *New Covenant* which Christ introduced to His followers superseded and essentially annulled the Covenants made previously with Israel. There is only one problem with this idea - *the New Covenant was not made with Gentiles!*

Look closely at the definition of the New Covenant as it is described in detail by the prophet Jeremiah:

> Behold, the days are coming, says the LORD, when I will make a new covenant with the house of Israel and the

---

318 Romans 11:25-27 RSV

> house of Judah, not like the covenant which I made with their fathers when I took them by the hand to bring them out of the land of Egypt, My covenant which they broke, though I was their Husband, says the LORD. But this is the covenant which I will make with the house of Israel after those days, says the LORD: I will put my law within them, and I will write it upon their hearts; and I will be their God, and they shall be My people. And no longer shall each man teach his neighbor and each his brother, saying, 'Know the LORD,' for they shall all know Me, from the least of them to the greatest, says the LORD; for I will forgive their iniquity, and I will remember their sin no more." 35 Thus says the LORD, who gives the sun for light by day and the fixed order of the moon and the stars for light by night, who stirs up the sea so that its waves roar--the LORD of hosts is His name: "If this fixed order departs from before me, says the LORD, then shall the descendants of Israel cease from being a nation before Me forever.[319][emphasis added]

Most Christians have been taught or have assumed that God made the Old Covenant with Israel and that Jesus forged the New Covenant with the Gentile nations. *That is not what you just read.* Read again the words I have underlined above, and you will see that the New Covenant was specifically made with the *people of Israel!* Even though a few Gentiles were touched by His ministry, Jesus declared plainly that He had come exclusively for the sake of the "lost house of Israel." He even forbade His disciples to go into the villages of the Gentiles.

> Go nowhere among the Gentiles, and enter no town of the Samaritans, but go rather to the lost sheep of the house of

[319] Jeremiah 31:31-36 RSV

> Israel.[320][emphasis added] And behold, a Canaanite woman from that region came out and cried, "Have mercy on me, O Lord, Son of David; my daughter is severely possessed by a demon." But He did not answer her a word. And His disciples came and begged Him, saying, "Send her away, for she is crying after us." He answered, "I was sent only to the lost sheep of the house of Israel." [321][emphasis added]

If no covenant has been made specifically with Gentiles then how did they become recipients of the New Covenant Jesus made with Israel? To answer that question, we must go back in time thousands of years to the days of Joseph.

Joseph's Egyptian-Born Sons

Joseph, one of the twelve sons of Jacob, was sold as a slave to Egypt by his brothers because of favoritism shown to him by their father. Through a series of circumstances, he eventually became the chief adviser to Pharaoh. Joseph's name means "The Lord shall add to me another son." The "other son" that the Lord added, as I will show, is the Gentile Church which has been "added" to the Covenant God made with Israel.

Because of his gift of interpreting dreams, Joseph was given a high position in Egypt and married an Egyptian woman named Asenath.[322] She bore Joseph two sons named Ephraim and Manasseh. It is important to note that these two sons were of *mixed blood,* being half Egyptian.

---

[320] Matthew 10:5-6 RSV
[321] Matthew 15:22-24 RSV
[322] See Genesis 46:20

The Blessing of Ephraim

When Jacob was nearing the time of his death, he wanted to bless his two grandsons. He asked Joseph to bring Ephraim and Manasseh to him. Joseph positioned Manasseh toward his father's right hand because he was the firstborn son and rightful heir to that special blessing. But when Jacob stretched out his hands to impart the patriarchal blessing, he did something unusual. He crossed his arms, literally forming the sign of the Cross, and laid his right hand upon the head of Ephraim. When Joseph saw that the younger was receiving the favored blessing, he tried to correct his father.

> Not so, my father; for this one is the first-born; put your right hand upon his head." But his father refused, and said, "I know, my son, I know; he also shall become a people, and he also shall be great; nevertheless his younger brother shall be greater than he, and his descendants shall become <u>a multitude of nations</u>." So he blessed them that day, saying, "By you Israel will pronounce blessings, saying, 'God make you as E'phraim and as Manas'seh'"; and thus he put E'phraim before Manas'seh.[323] [emphasis added]

A Multitude of Nations

Notice that the blessing given to Ephraim was that he would become a "multitude of nations" (Hebrew *milo 'gowy).* The words of this blessing are very important, but to fully understand them we must leave them here for now and go ahead in time to the days of King Solomon.

---

[323] Genesis 48:18-20 RSV

Solomon's Divided Kingdom

After the reign of Solomon came to an end, Israel became a divided kingdom. God was displeased with Solomon because he had erred by practicing idolatry.[324] Upon his death, the kingdom was divided into northern and southern territories. The king of the northern kingdom was named Jeroboam. The Bible describes him as an "Ephraimite."[325] His domain was comprised of ten tribes and was known as the Kingdom of Ephraim.

Rehoboam, Solomon's actual son, reigned over the southern kingdom, which included the two remaining tribes of Judah and Benjamin. Since Judah was the dominant tribe, Judah and Benjamin together were called the Kingdom of Judah.

The capital of the northern kingdom was the city Tirzah, and the capital of the southern kingdom remained Jerusalem. In the *Song of Songs*, Solomon compares his bride to these two important cities.

> Thou art beautiful, O my love, as **Tirzah**, comely as **Jerusalem**, terrible as an army with banners.[326][emphasis added]

When we consider that this was written *before* his kingdom was actually divided, we realize that Solomon was foretelling, not only the *division* of his kingdom into two parts, but also her future restoration (as the Bride) at the end of the age! *Amazing!*

The Kingdom of Ephraim

Even though the kingdoms were divided, Jews from the

---

[324] 1 Kings 11:4

[325] I Kings 11:26, 28

[326] Song of Songs 6:4 KJV

northern kingdom still traveled south to Jerusalem during the holy feast days. Jeroboam, fearing his tribes might defect back to Rehoboam, instituted a religion similar to Judaism but with its own traditions, priesthood and two golden calves to serve as gods. As you can imagine, his idolatry thrust the northern kingdom into spiritual decline and ultimate apostasy.[327] Eventually, in 718 BC, God allowed Assyria to attack and conquer the ten tribes. The Jews were deported from their homeland and made slaves. As time passed, they were sold to other nations and dispersed to the four corners of the known world. The prophet Hosea confirmed this when he said, "Ephraim, hath mixed himself among the people."[328]

The blood of Ephraim, which began as the *mixed bloodline* of the offspring of Joseph and Asenath, was diluted even more as the ten tribes scattered among the nations, intermarried, and had children. The end result of the dispersion was that the ten tribes eventually lost their national identity. Even today, they are referred to as the "lost" tribes of Israel.

The Kingdom of Judah

Just like the northern kingdom, the southern kingdom of Judah also ultimately proved unfaithful to God. God chastened them as well, but they did not suffer the same fate as Ephraim. Instead of being dispersed among the nations, they were taken as slaves to Babylon, where they served for seventy years. This period of exile was during the time of Daniel. Afterward, during the days of Ezra, they were given permission by King Cyrus to return to Jerusalem to rebuild their Temple and city. Because they were not dispersed, as were the tribes of Ephraim, Judah was able

---

[327] 1 Kings 12:30-31
[328] Hosea 7:8 KJV

to maintain their national identity as God's people. This is in keeping with the promise given to Judah, which says:

> The **sceptre** shall not depart from Judah…[329] [emphasis added]

Judah went to Babylon as Jews and returned to Jerusalem as Jews. They maintained their national identity, bloodline, and traditions, which identify them still today as God's special people.

A Blessing or a Curse?

Orthodox Jews have a tradition in which grandparents lay their hands on the heads of their grandchildren and bless them according to Genesis 48:16. They speak the blessing, "May God make you like Ephraim and Manasseh." Considering the fact that Ephraim grew so wicked that God expelled them from the land and scattered them among the nations, this seems like an unusual thing to wish upon one's grandchild! It seems more like a curse than a blessing *unless* it refers to a *future* blessing. Consider the words of the prophet Ezekiel concerning Ephraim's ultimate destiny:

> Thus says the Lord God, "Behold, I will take the sons of Israel from among the nations where they have gone, and I will gather them from every side and bring them into their own land; and I will make them one nation in the land, on the mountains of Israel; and one king will be king for all of them; and they will no longer be two nations (Ephraim and Judah), and they will no longer be divided into two kingdoms (Ephraim and Judah), "And they will no longer defile themselves with their idols, or with their detestable

[329] Genesis 49:10

> things, or with any of their transgressions; but I will deliver them from all their dwelling places in which they have sinned, and will cleanse them. And they will be My people, and I will be their God.[330]

God's covenant has always been with the bloodline of Abraham, and the promise was that through him *all nations* would be blessed![331] In order to accomplish this, God began a plan to include the Gentiles into the covenant which He had made *exclusively* with the Jews. He did this by disseminating the blood of Abraham *into* all the families of the earth!

Placement Theology

Consider the unsearchable wisdom of God in how He did not alter His Covenant with Israel in order to make it conform to the Gentiles; instead, He altered the *Gentiles* to make *them* conform to His Covenant! God's "mystery plan" to graft the Gentiles into the Jewish Covenant began when Joseph had two mixed-blood sons with his Egyptian wife. By God's election, Ephraim was chosen to be the recipient of the firstborn blessing. Ephraim's mixed bloodline (Jew and Gentile) grew into a dominant tribe. When an Ephraimite (Jeroboam) became the ruler of ten of the Jewish tribes, the blood became even *more* diluted. And finally, when the ten tribes of the Kingdom of Ephraim were taken captive by Assyria and scattered across the whole world, the blood of Abraham began to infiltrate into the nations. Over thousands of years, the exponential rate at which the bloodline has traveled and intermingled with the nations is now utterly pervasive. It is here that Replacement Theology fails to recognize the fact that God did not set Israel aside in order to establish

---

[330] Ezekiel 37:21-23 NAS
[331] Genesis 12:3

Gentiles in His plan. He simply added Gentiles into Israel by grafting them into the bloodline.

Esther or Haddaseh

Queen Esther provides a beautiful picture of Gentile believers being brought into the Jewish covenant. Esther was a queen with two names (two natures). Her Persian name was Esther, but her Jewish name was Haddaseh. Even though she was a Jewess, she was thought to be a Persian (Gentile) by all except her uncle Mordecai. She went before the King as a "Gentile" to intercede for the deliverance of the Jews. In fact, it was her presumed status as a Gentile that granted her proximity and intimate access to the King. Consider that it is those who are of the tribes of Ephraim and who represent the "Gentile" Church today who faithfully support and intercede for the protection and deliverance of Israel from her enemies! The greatest friend Israel has in the world is the Church of Jesus Christ! It's not until the very end of Esther's story that her true Jewish nature is revealed. And so it will be at the end of the age, when the true Jewish nature of the Gentile Church will be clearly understood.

The Wild Olive Tree

In the book of Romans, the Apostle Paul uses the analogy of two olive trees to show how God has conformed the Gentiles in order to include them in His redemptive plan. He refers to them as a "wild olive tree" as compared with Israelites, who are a cultivated tree. In describing the process of inclusion, Paul says it was as if God broke branches off of the cultivated olive tree (Israel) in order to graft a branch from the wild olive tree (Gentiles) into the original plant. Keep in mind that in the passage below, Paul is speaking to the Church at Rome, comprised predominantly of Gentile believers who had come to believe that God had set aside the Jews.

> But if some of the branches [of Israel] were broken off, and you, [Gentiles] a wild olive shoot, were grafted in their place to share the richness of the olive tree, do not boast over the branches. If you do boast, remember it is not you that support the root, but the root that supports you. You will say, "Branches were broken off so that I might be grafted in." That is true. They were broken off because of their unbelief, but you stand fast only through faith. So do not become proud, but stand in awe. For if God did not spare the natural branches, neither will he spare you.[332]

The wild olive branches did not *replace* the root; they were merely *added to* the root by grafting them in. Rather than *replacing* Israel, the Church has simply been *placed into* Israel! Notice too that Paul refers to the Gentiles as a "wild olive tree." In the Bible, the olive tree is a symbol reserved for Israel.[333] Paul's use of the term "wild" olive tree is a way of describing the *nature* of the Gentile believers. God did not cultivate the Gentiles as He did the Jews. They grew wild and untamed without God's Law, His prophets, or His presence in their midst. Yet God gave them equal status by calling them an olive tree, albeit a wild variety. When grafting plants, it is imperative that the genus of the plants is compatible. For instance, it is possible to graft different varieties of apples onto a single apple tree root so that the single tree is capable of bearing different varieties of apples. Among plants of differing genera, however, a graft is highly improbable. So, when the Apostle Paul uses the imagery of a cultivated and a wild olive tree being grafted together, he is suggesting that this is possible

---

[332] Romans 11:17-21 RSV

[333] Hosea 14:6, See also Psalm 52:8 and Psalm 128:3

only because both trees are of the same stock! The Church has not replaced Israel. The Church has become a vital part of Israel!

The Meaning of "The Fullness of the Gentiles"

The blessing given to Ephraim stated that he would become a "multitude of nations."[334] The Hebrew words translated "multitude of nations" are *melo'gowy,* and they are most literally rendered as the "fullness of the Gentiles!" With this understanding, consider the following words of the Apostle Paul:

> ..."that blindness in part has happened to Israel until the fullness of the Gentiles (multitude of nations) has come in, and so all Israel will be saved, as it is written: "The Deliverer will come out of Zion, and He will turn away ungodliness from Jacob.[335][emphasis added]

In the past, we have read these words and thought they meant that God was dealing with the Gentiles *until* the last Gentile was saved. Then He would begin saving Jews. This interpretation perpetuates the misconception that God has replaced Israel with the Church and that a wall of separation still exists between the two. It really means that Israel is not *complete* until the full number of Gentile believers has been added to her. "All Israel" is not made up of Jews alone. "All Israel" is comprised of both the house of Judah (Jews) and the house of Ephraim (Gentiles.)

The Spirit of Error

Like all truth, the "mystery of the Gentiles" has been

---

[334] See Genesis 48:18-20

[335] Romans 11:25-26

twisted to conform to the prejudices of some who are either anti-Semitic or who have illogically arrived at the conclusion that God has rejected Israel and nullified His covenant with her. Some have taught something called British Israelism, which is the preposterous belief that people of Western European descent are the direct descendants of the ten lost tribes of Israel. According to this line of thinking, the British throne is the seat of the Davidic kingdom. This is not only ridiculous but it is Replacement Theology at its worst! Other less scholarly thinkers have even hijacked this truth to somehow try to prove the supremacy of the white race, a concept that belies all rational thinking.

Honest Skeptics

On the other hand, some are honestly skeptical of the idea that Ephraim was God's plan to include the Gentiles in the covenant of Israel. They argue that if the Gentiles are considered part of the house of Israel, then it becomes meaningless to be a Jew. Everyone, in essence, has become a Jew! They see this as just another way of replacing Israel with the Church. While I understand this concern, I believe it is an unfounded fear. Suppose a couple who already have a natural born child decide to adopt another child. They don't *replace* their natural born child with their adopted child. Neither do they set the plans they have made for their natural child aside in deference to the adopted child. Both children become part of the family. The grafting of the Gentiles into the house of Israel does not lessen the individual significance of the Jews, nor does it alter God's plan for them as a chosen vessel for His purposes. Those specific purposes can be seen today in the way God is restoring Jews to the land of Israel. *But even the re-gathering is not for Jews alone!*

The Second Re-gathering

Presently, most Gentile believers feel no special calling to return to the land of Israel. *At least not yet!* While much has been written and said about the prophetic return of Jews to the Promised Land, the Bible speaks of a *second return* that will take place as well. The "second return" will be Gentile believers who have been grafted into the Covenants God made with Israel! In the future, Israel will experience a massive influx of Christians who will return to the physical land and join with the house of Jacob. When this occurs, the present borders of Israel will strain under the sheer number of people who will gather there. Consider the words of Zechariah:

> Jerusalem shall be inhabited as villages without walls, because of the multitude of men and cattle in it. [5] For I will be to her a wall of fire round about, says the LORD, and I will be the glory within her.[336][emphasis added]

After God has saved the tents of Judah (Jews) first,[337] then He will call for people from *all nations* to gather in Jerusalem for the drama of the end of the age!

> Ho! ho! Flee from the land of the north, says the LORD; for I have spread you abroad as the four winds of the heavens says the LORD. Ho! Escape to Zion, you who dwell with the daughter of Babylon.[338]

Remember, Judah was taken to Babylon for seventy years

---

[336] Zechariah 2:45 RSV

[337] In Zechariah 12:7, the prophet Zechariah said that God would save "the tents of Judah first." By using the term "first," the implication is that others will follow.

[338] Zechariah 2:6-7 RSV

and then returned. It was the northern Kingdom of Ephraim that was dispersed to become the "multitude of the nations"[339] (lit. "fullness of the Gentiles" *melo'gowy*). Look at what Isaiah says:

> It shall come to pass in that day, That the Lord shall set his hand again the second time to recover the remnant of His people who are left, from Assyria and Egypt, from Pathros, and Cush, from Elam, and Shinar, From Hamath, and the islands of the sea. He will set up a banner for the nations, And will assemble the outcasts of Israel, and gather together the dispersed of Judah From the four corners of the earth. Also the envy of Ephraim shall depart, And the adversaries of Judah shall be cut off; Ephraim shall not envy Judah, and Judah shall not harass Ephraim.[340][emphasis added]

Ten Men and One Jew

While most Gentile believers feel no prompting to make Israel their home at the present time, the Bible is clear that this *will* happen. In the following verses from Zechariah we read the phrase, "people shall YET come," indicating a delay between the time the Jews begin returning to Israel and when *other* people will gather there.

> Thus says the LORD of hosts: Peoples shall ***yet*** come, even the inhabitants of many cities; the inhabitants of one city shall go to another, saying, 'Let us go at once to entreat the favor of the LORD, and to seek the LORD of hosts; I am going.' ***Many peoples and strong nations*** shall come to seek the LORD of hosts in Jerusalem, and to entreat the

---

[339] Genesis 48:18-20
[340] Isaiah 11:11-13

> favor of the LORD. Thus says the LORD of hosts: In those days ***ten men from the nations of every tongue*** shall take hold of the robe of a Jew, saying, 'Let us go with you, for we have heard that God is with you.[341][emphasis added]

Remember, Ephraim was comprised of ten of the twelve tribes of Israel who were dispersed and assimilated into every nation of the world. The "ten men" from every nation and tongue who take hold of the robe of a Jew represent the returning ten tribes of Ephraim - the Gentile believers being rejoined to their brothers the Jews in the land of their inheritance! What a glorious day this describes, when God not only restores Judah to her homeland; but also calls the dispersed of Ephraim from the four corners of the world. Ephraim (the Gentile son who was added to the house of Israel)[342] and Judah (the natural born Jewish son) will lay down their differences. Read those same verses from the MESSAGE version of the Bible:

> And He'll raise that rallying banner high, visible to all nations, gather in all the scattered exiles of Israel, Pull in all the dispersed refugees of Judah from the four winds and the seven seas. The jealousy of Ephraim will dissolve, the hostility of Judah will vanish—Ephraim no longer the jealous rival of Judah, Judah no longer the hostile rival of Ephraim! ***Blood brothers united***...[343] [emphasis added]

At that time, the demolishing of the wall of separation between Jew and Gentile made possible by the Cross of Christ will become a living reality! Consider also that Jesus said:

---

[341] Zechariah 8:20-23 RSV
[342] Joseph's name means "the Lord shall ADD to me ANOTHER son"
[343] Isaiah 11:12-16 THE MESSAGE

> ...other sheep I have, which are not of this fold; them also I must bring, and they will hear My voice; and there will be <u>one flock, and one shepherd</u>.[344][emphasis added]

The high priest, Caiaphas, even prophesied that Jesus had to die - not only for the sake of the Jewish nation - but also for <u>*all the children of God (Ephraim) who were scattered abroad*</u>*!*[345]

Two Olive Trees

The prophet Zechariah saw a vision of two olive trees which were standing before the Lord. He saw that they fed their oil into a common lamp-stand which became a singular flame. When Zechariah asked who these two olive trees were, he was told that they were "the two anointed ones that stand by the LORD of the whole earth."[346]

I believe these two olive trees are the same olive trees used by the Apostle Paul as an analogy to represent the Jews and the Church. The Jews are the cultivated olive tree, and the Gentile believers are the wild olive tree. In Paul's analogy, the two trees are grafted together to become one tree. In the book of Revelation, John saw a similar vision of two olive trees. This time, however, the two trees are described as "two witnesses."

> And I will give power to my two witnesses, and they will prophesy one thousand two hundred and sixty days, (three and a half years) clothed in sackcloth. <u>These are the two olive trees, and the two lamp-stands standing before the God of the earth.</u>[347] [emphasis added]

---

[344] John 10:16
[345] John 11:49-52
[346] Zechariah 4:14
[347] Revelation 11:3-4

These two witnesses are given supernatural power to prophesy during the final three and a half years of the reign of the Antichrist. After that time, they are overcome and killed. Then, after three days, they are raised from the dead in the sight of all people and taken up into Heaven. Much speculation has been given to the identity of these two witnesses. Some think they are Moses and Elijah. Others have suggested Enoch and Elijah. Could it be that they represent two *companies* of people rather than two individual persons? There are only two "witnesses" in the world today who testify of the one true God - Ephraim and Judah! *Christianity and Judaism!*

The Messianic Seal

The image below is called the "Messianic Seal." It is one of the most prominent symbols used by the early Christian Church. Many of these seals were discovered in the ruins of a church located near King David's tomb. The Seal shows clearly that the early Christians understood the inter-relatedness of the Church to Israel. The Church, represented by the fish symbol at the bottom of the seal, is integrated into the Star of David and the two of them merge into one lamp-stand, called a menorah. They are *two olive trees pouring their oil into one common lamp!*

The Messianic Seal

18

AN END-TIME PARADIGM

When these things begin to take place, stand up and lift your heads, because your redemption is drawing near.
The Gospel of Luke

Signs in Heaven and on Earth

The Bridal revelation is not complete without a close look at the events which will unfold during the Last Days. In this chapter, I will present a simple template for the major events as they might possibly occur in the final days ahead.

> He delivers and rescues, He works **signs and wonders in Heaven and on earth**...[348]

We are living at a time in history like no other. God is working signs in heaven and earth. On earth, the Jews are once again living in their homeland after almost two thousand years of exile. This fulfillment of Bible prophecy in our lifetime is a major sign on earth! Heaven too is sending us undeniable signals that mankind's days are numbered. In the Old Testament, the prophet Joel said the moon would turn to blood as a sign leading up to the day of the Lord.[349] Mark Biltz, pastor of El Shaddai Ministries in

---

[348] Daniel 6:27 RSV
[349] See Joel 2:31

Bonney Lake, Washington, made a startling discovery relating to "blood moons." While visiting the official website of NASA,[350] he found that beginning in 2008 through 2015, a rare astronomical phenomena, called a *lunar tetrad* would occur - not once - but a total of six times! The word "tetrad" means a "set of four," and so a lunar tetrad occurs when four total lunar eclipses happen in succession. What makes this interesting is that a total lunar eclipse is called a "blood moon," because the moon appears rusty red during the eclipse. Even more intriguing is that these blood moons will all occur on God's holy Feast days! How rare is this? The last time tetrads were seen was in 1967-68, coinciding with the Six Day War, when Jerusalem was recaptured by Jewish forces! Before that, tetrads occurred right after Israel became a nation, in 1949-50! Strangely, however, before 1949, there were no occurrences of tetrads going all the way back to the sixteenth century! The manner in which these tetrads will be occurring in clusters from the years 2008 through 2015 is exceptional to our generation! I am not suggesting that Jesus will return by the year 2015. On the other hand, these are certainly signs in the heavens that should not be ignored.

A Paradigm of Events

What *is* certain is that on some future Feast of Trumpets known only by the Father, Jesus *will* return to earth, sweep His Bride off of her feet, and carry her back to His Father's house where the Marriage of the Lamb will take place. At the conclusion of the ceremony, Jesus will escort His *Beloved* to their "bridal chamber" where they will reside undisturbed for seven years. Meanwhile, on earth, the stage will be set for mankind's final days.

---

[350] National Aeronautics and Space Administration (NASA)

With the Rapture of the Bride having taken place, the Church that is left behind will prepare to take her appointed place in the drama that is about to unfold. With the prospect of persecution and even martyrdom now a very real certainty, those who have lived a lukewarm, superficial Christian life will flee the Church en mass. The Apostle Paul refers to this event as the "apostasy."[351] The people who will remain after this mass defection from the faith will comprise a holy assembly of men and women who, like the followers of Jesus in the first century, will bravely embrace the crown of persecution and death. They are described by the prophet Daniel in the following passage:

> Those who have insight among the people will give understanding to the many; yet they will fall by the sword and by flame, by captivity and plunder for many days.[352]

The controversy that exists in the Church regarding the Rapture is based on an "either/or" presumption. *Either* the Church is taken out of the world before the Tribulation begins *or* the Church is called to endure the Tribulation. A third possibility exists, however. If the Church and the Bride are *not* the same, then *both* scenarios become both possible and plausible. The Bride is removed *before* the Tribulation, and the Church goes *through* the Tribulation, *at least the first half of it.*

Daniel says the Antichrist will seek to "wear out the saints of the Most High"[353] by waging a campaign of terror against them. Jesus affirmed this fact as well.

---

[351] 1 Thessalonians 2:3
[352] Daniel 11:33 NASB
[353] Daniel 7:25 KJV

> Brother will deliver up brother to death, and the father his child, and children will rise against parents and have them put to death; and you will be hated by all for my name's sake. But he who endures to the end will be saved.[354]

This false Messiah will infiltrate the Church with spies who will betray believers to the authorities.

> Now when they fall they will be granted a little help, and many will join with them in hypocrisy.[355]

While no one can fully explain all the reasons why God will call His Church to walk through the fire of suffering and even death, we are told that the *purpose* of the fire is to *refine* the saints and make them ready for the end.

> ...and some of those who are wise shall fall, *to refine and to cleanse them and to make them white,* until the time of the end, for it is yet for the time appointed.[356]

In contrast to this, the Bride has no need to be purified by tribulation fire because she will have *already* been refined by a fire: *the intimate, vehement fire of her Bridegroom's love.* She will discern beforehand the nearness of the coming of her Bridegroom, and she will diligently prepare herself for it.

> Let us rejoice and exult and give Him the glory, for the marriage of the Lamb has come, and His Bride has made herself ready; it was granted her to be clothed with fine linen, bright and pure -- for the fine linen is the righteous

[354] Matthew 10:21-22 RSV
[355] Daniels 11:34 NASB
[356] Daniel 11:35 RSV

deeds of the saints. And the angel said to me, "Write this: Blessed are those who are invited to the marriage supper of the Lamb".[357] [emphasis added]

Blow the Trumpet

The blowing of trumpets is significant to three Jewish feasts: The Feast of Pentecost, the Feast of Trumpets and the Day of Atonement.

The Feast of Pentecost is known as the **First Trumpet**. The Jews believe that God gave the Law to Moses on the Feast of Pentecost, so the "first trump" celebrates the first time the marvelous words of the Torah were heard. It is interesting that on the day of Pentecost, when Moses delivered the Law to the Israelites, three thousand men died because of the sin of the golden calf.[358] When the Holy Spirit was given to the Church (also on the Feast of Pentecost), three thousand souls *were saved!* [359] "The letter [Law] kills but the Spirit gives life!"[360]

The second time the trumpets were blown was on the Feast of Trumpets called, *Yom Teruah*. This feast is known as the **Last Trumpet** because it signaled the *last chance* for the Jews to repent before the Day of Atonement (Judgment) arrived. Ten days elapsed between the Feast of Trumpets and the Day of Atonement. These ten days are called the *Days of Awe,* when the people are admonished to humble themselves and ponder their lives during the past year.

The third feast where trumpets were blown was the Day of Atonement. It was called the day of the **"Great Trump"** or the *Shofar HaGadol*.

---

357 Revelation 19:7-9 RSV
358 Exodus 32:28
359 Acts 2:41
360 2 Corinthians 3:6

The Sound of the Rapture

The first trump of the Christian era sounded on the Feast of Pentecost two thousand years ago and was described as a "mighty rushing wind" coming down from heaven. In the Greek language "mighty rushing wind" is rendered *pherō biaios pnoē* and means "an announcement that is forced out by the breath." That perfectly describes the blowing of a shofar! The next trumpet blast that will be heard from Heaven will occur when Jesus comes for His Bride on a future Feast of Trumpets!

> For the Lord Himself will descend from heaven with a cry of command, with the archangel's call, and **with the sound of the trumpet of God**. And the dead in Christ will rise first, then we who are alive, who are left, shall be caught up together with them in the clouds to meet the Lord in the air; and so we shall always be with the Lord.[361][emphasis added]

For the Bride, the shofar blast will call her to her wedding. For the rest of the world, the sound of the trump will be a warning that soon everyone will have to stand before God and answer for their sins.

The "Trigger" of the Tribulation

The Rapture of the Bride will be the singular event that will signal the arrival of the final seven years of the world's existence. It is the "trigger" of the Tribulation. Shortly after the Bride is removed from the earth, the "man of lawlessness"[362] will

---

[361] 1 Thessalonians 4:16 RSV

[362] 1 Thessalonians 2:3 "the man of lawlessness" is another term that describes the Satanic figure known as the Antichrist.

step onto the world stage. At first he will not be seen as the embodiment of pure evil that he truly is. Instead, he will take the world by popular storm as he systematically ushers in an era of unparalleled prosperity and diplomacy. In the book of Revelation, he is personified as a rider on a white horse. He carries a bow but no arrows, indicating that he arrives as a man of peace.[363] He will win the world's approval and adulation by means of his cunning and magnetic personality. As part of his plan, he will forge a treaty with the nations of the world in regard to Israel and her Middle Eastern neighbors, something that no leader before him has been able to do. As part of the terms of this unholy compact, the Jews will be allowed to rebuild their Temple. Meanwhile, an authentic outpouring of the Holy Spirit will be breaking out among Messianic Jews and Christians who will be gathering together from all over the world to restore the Tabernacle of David!

The prophet Amos foretold this event:

> "In that day I will raise up the booth of David that is fallen and repair its breaches, and raise up its ruins, and rebuild it as in the days of old; that they may possess the remnant of Edom and <u>all the nations who are called by my name</u>," says the LORD who does this.[364][emphasis added]

Note that the restoration of the Tabernacle of David will be accomplished - not by Jews alone - but by all the nations (lit. גוי *gowy* meaning Gentiles)!

---

[363] Revelation 6:2
[364] Amos 9:11-12 RSV

Two Tabernacles

To fully understand the significance of this, we must remember that when David pitched his Tabernacle at Mt. Zion, the Tabernacle of Moses was still in operation on top of Mt. Gibeon.[365] There were two tabernacles operating at the same time! And even though the Ark of the Covenant had fallen into the hands of the Philistines, that did not stop the priests from going through the ritual of worship which included daily blood sacrifices.

When David's Tabernacle is rebuilt at the end of time, it will also be pitched in the shadow of the third Temple of the Jews. When the systematic mechanics of Levitical worship are once again employed at the Temple site, God will provide a witness of *true worship* in Spirit and truth in David's restored tent! Once again, two tabernacles will be functioning at the same time. One will minister meaningless ritual while the other is alive with the Spirit of God!

The Abomination of Desolation

Once the blood of bulls and goats actually begins to run upon the altar of the third Temple, the outcry of animal rights activists who "worship and serve the **creature** more than the Creator"[366] will be deafening. Jerusalem will truly become "a cup of trembling" for the whole world and problematic for the Antichrist as well. Unable to dissuade the Jews to end their slaughter of animals, he will be forced to end Temple worship by the use of military force.

> And arms [military] shall stand on his part, and they shall pollute the sanctuary of strength, and shall take away the

[365] See 1 Chronicles 1:3 and 1 Chronicles 16:39
[366] Romans 1:25

> daily sacrifice, and they shall place the **abomination** that maketh desolate.[367] [emphasis added]

In so doing, his true satanic nature will finally be revealed to the Jews. When this happens they, along with their Christian brothers, will have to flee.

> Therefore when you see *the abomination of desolation*, spoken of by Daniel the prophet, standing in the holy place, (whoever reads, let him understand) then let those who are in Judaea flee to the mountains: Let him who is on the housetop not go down to take anything out of his house. And let him who is in the field not go back to get his clothes. But woe to those that are pregnant and to those who are nursing babies in those days! And pray that your flight may not be in winter, neither on the Sabbath. For then there will be great tribulation, such as has not been since the beginning of the world until this time, no, nor ever shall be.[368]

Those who do not escape will face almost certain martyrdom as the wrath of the Antichrist is unleashed upon those who follow Jesus. Thus begins the final three and a half years of time called the "time of Jacob's trouble,"[369] when the judgments of God are unleashed upon the world and all those who follow the Beast.

---

[367] Daniel 11:31 KJV
[368] Matthew 24:15-21
[369] Jeremiah 30:7

Answering the Call

Those who answer the call to *Become the Beloved* will escape what is to come. But what of those who do not? The last of the seven churches to be addressed in the book of Revelation is the Church at Laodicea. Laodicea represents the Church that has a form of godliness but no power or reality; a lamp but no oil. Jesus stands *outside* the door of this church and knocks.[370]

In the *Song*, there is a parallel scene in which the Shulamite dreams that Solomon is standing outside her door - knocking and seeking entrance.

> I slept, but my heart was awake. Hark! my beloved is knocking. "Open to me, my sister, my love, my dove, my perfect one; for my head is wet with dew, my locks with the drops of the night." I had put off my garment, how could I put it on? I had bathed my feet, how could I soil them?[371]

I believe this is a picture of the Church in the Last Days being summoned to arouse from her slumber and become the Bride of Christ. Many will be unmoved by the Bridegroom's appeal. Running after Him will require more than they are willing to give. When the unresponsive Church finally *does* realize the urgency of the hour, it will be too late:

> I [finally] opened to my beloved, but my beloved had turned and gone. My soul failed me when he spoke. I sought him, but found him not; I called him, but he gave no answer. The watchmen found me, as they went about in the city; they beat me, they wounded me, they took away

---

[370] Revelation 3:20

[371] Song of Songs 5:2-3 RSV

my mantle, those watchmen of the walls.[372]

Before these events unfold, the Bride will go to be with her Beloved. The Church, however, will be caught unprepared and left behind. Her mantle will be stripped away and she will become prey to the "watchmen."

Even now, the Church is being invited to arise and become the Bride of Christ. A remnant will answer this call. Others will cling to the predictable comfort of the status quo of "religion without relationship," thus sealing their fate.

---

[372] Song of Songs 5:6-7 RSV

AFTERWORD

And who knows whether you have not come to the kingdom for such a time as this?
The Book of Esther

Becoming the Beloved is both a personal as well as a corporate experience. In the book of Revelation, the Bride is portrayed as a city indwelt by the Lamb.[373] The Bridal revelation exists both in the *micro* and in the *macro* of the Kingdom of God. In the *micro,* it is all about you and me as individuals with worth and value to God. But it's also much bigger than just our own personal relationship with Him.

Like Queen Esther, the Bride of Christ is being raised up "for such a time as this," for the specific purpose of going before her King to intercede for the protection and destiny of the Jews. The Church has been both the worst enemy and the best friend Israel has ever had. At its worst, the symbol of the Cross was hijacked and used by Adolph Hitler as the twisted rationale for the extermination of more than six million people.[374] Today we are only a generation removed from the time when this false and repugnant perversion of true Christianity was used as a weapon against the Jewish people. At its best, there is no greater friend to the people of Israel than Christians around the world who support her with prayer and financial gifts. Satan's diabolical hatred for the Jews, as it was manifested through Hitler, was only a dress rehearsal for what will occur at the end of days. Every nation of the world will be roused against the land of Israel and her people

---

[373] Revelation chapter 21

[374] The number of 6 million is based on the testimony of Adolf Eichmann at the Nuremberg Tribunal in 1946, however, Jews were not the only targets of Hitler and so, the total number of people murdered is probably much greater.

as Jerusalem is made a "cup of trembling for all nations."[375]

The story of Esther is a prophetic picture of the Bride of Christ uniquely called and chosen to be a vessel of intercession for the Jewish people in their time of greatest need. Even now, as the Bride of Christ is beginning to come forth in the earth, the "times of the Gentiles" is coming to an end. When the events I have shared about in this book begin to unfold, they will do so quickly. It may be only weeks or months away. On the other hand, it could still take years to be accomplished. It may be in my lifetime or in a generation yet to be. The signs of the times, however, would indicate that it will be sooner and not later. As the Church age wanes, a spiritual awakening will be birthed in the hearts of Jews worldwide. When the Bride of Christ is taken from the earth, she will go immediately into the very presence of her King. Once there, like Esther, she will accomplish her intercession for Israel *face to face*.

Today, men and women worldwide are awakening to the call to *Become the Beloved.* My prayer is that this book will help you answer that call.

---

[375] Zechariah 12:2 [paraphrase]

OTHER BOOKS BY MARK

Breaking the Seal is a comprehensive verse-by-verse study of the Song of Solomon.

Available at:
www.shulamiteministries.org